WHAT PEOPLE ARE SAYING ABOUT

WITHOUT YOU THERE: THE ZEN OF UNITY

Paramananda takes on the challenge of articulating the non-dual, which is often conveyed in an overly holy, very serious, and impersonal way, and fills it with humor, humanness, and user-friendly accessibility, with bright gems of wisdom strewn throughout. A beautiful book.

Mariana Caplan, PhD, Psychotherapist and author of *Eyes Wide Open: Cultivating Discernment on the Spiritual Path* and *Halfway Up the Mountain: The Error of Premature Claims to Enlightenment*

The author's unique blend of conversational language, frequent comic relief, and lack of grand declarations makes it easy for the ego's defensive wall to drop, allowing for any reader to recognize who they truly are.

Noah Elkrief, author of *A Guide to The Present Moment*

This book makes it easy to see straight into the heart of truth. Often the spiritual path can seem unclear and cluttered. Paramananda is not only entertaining but direct, removing each obstacle until what remains is a simple path to Unity.

Dr. Susan Shumsky, author of *Divine Revelation*

In *Without You There* Paramananda expresses the absolute truth in simple words, speaking it directly out of his aliveness and joy of realization. With insight and intuition, he acts as a channel transferring universal information.

Andrea Scarsi Msc.D., aut   *Science* and *Secrets of Meditation*

Without You There: The Zen of Unity

Without You There: The Zen of Unity

Paramananda Ishaya

MANTRA BOOKS

Winchester, UK
Washington, USA

First published by Mantra Books, 2014
Mantra Books is an imprint of John Hunt Publishing Ltd., Laurel House, Station Approach,
Alresford, Hants, SO24 9JH, UK
office1@jhpbooks.net
www.johnhuntpublishing.com
www.mantra-books.net

For distributor details and how to order please visit the 'Ordering' section on our website.

Text copyright: Paramananda Ishaya 2013

ISBN: 978 1 78279 479 0

A CIP catalogue record for this book is available from the British Library.

Design: Stuart Davies
www.stuartdaviesart.com

Printed in the USA by Edwards Brothers Malloy

We operate a distinctive and ethical publishing philosophy in all
areas of our business, from our global network of authors to
production and worldwide distribution.

CONTENTS

This book is dedicated to all the Teachers, Students and Monks that have made me laugh and cry with Joy.

Acknowledgements

To Drew Schumacher: Your work editing *Without You There* is excellent. I loved all of our apparently "enlightening" talks at the coffee shop. You have a super character or "monkey suit", as you once put it.

The End

Okay we have made it to the end; we can all go home now.

Unlike a normal book we are starting from the end because Unity works backwards to the usual forward thinking of the world. We want to go back to the source, back to where we came from do we not?

This is like sitting in your favorite chair at home and dreaming of a tropical vacation paradise on a beach; you are not aware you are sitting on the chair anymore... you are no longer aware you are in your home... you are swimming in the ocean and feeling the warm sand on your feet. Suddenly the phone rings and you snap out of it. 'You' get called back and realize that you are still sitting on the chair in your home. You left home to go to the beach, but did you actually leave? No of course not. You are already home.

Unity is seeing that you are already home and having the same satisfaction of the warm sand on your feet and the ocean on your side without having to get up from your chair.

We become so accustomed to thinking in certain ways that we tend to let it color every area of life. This way of thinking is reinforced by a variety of worldly programs, such as those seen on TV. Some of them we are aware of and others remain hidden until the obvious is seen. This thinking-ness – which obscures the obvious – then gets projected onto achieving the highest goal of Unity.

Unity is the dismantling of this way of thinking to reveal what is already here, there, everywhere and nowhere. By seeing the obvious we automatically see through these programs. This does not make them disappear in a cloud of dust necessarily but lessens their stranglehold over our Bliss.

These programs are not 'bad', some of them can even be entertaining, but being at the mercy of these we appear to be lost.

Have you watched the TV series *Lost*? I don't want to give it away but basically you are entertained but lost, just like reality, which is perhaps why the program was so successful. Yep that's me, lost. At least we can laugh about it.

Unity is not grey, blue, or even white; it is colorless and works in the opposite direction to what we think it would. Even if we have been trained in all the ancient knowledges and by the greatest of teachers, it still is not what we think it is. It is in another realm altogether, which is why the program is called *Lost*, not found.

In the realm of spirituality we soon discover that the ways of the past are no longer useful. To explore another possibility becomes not only exciting but also necessary if we are to see through the old habits and tricks of the mind.

The question is: Are you willing to see differently or to be wrong even if you strongly think you are right? If you knew that you would have everything you ever wanted, I am sure you would gladly be wrong. Most of us, however, stubbornly cling to our positions and beliefs because to us they represent truth, and over time these 'truths' become valued treasures. Reality does not work like this because it has nothing to do with belief or 'perceived' truths. It does not care what you think! It does not care whether or not you are close to your goal. It does not care if you understand a single thing!

A rare few see that this way of holding positions and beliefs no longer serves our interests or is even possible if we are to see into the true nature of things.

The possibility of Unity is hardly ever seen even though it is in plain sight.

To see it as a possibility is the first step. More often than not it is dismissed as too rare or hard to achieve and more than anything simply misunderstood. Perhaps it sounds too abstract or it is reserved for those highly spiritual ones we have heard or read about. It is for the saint or sage but not for little old me who works at the Gap, is a painter or dare I say a Lawyer. (Well maybe not a lawyer.)

There are many ideas around this subject, and the fact is all of them are wrong!

Unity's rarity is not because it is difficult to attain or because it is for the special few. It is rare because it is too simple and obvious for the human mind to comprehend. A genius is no closer or further than a simple fool. In some ways the fool is closer since the intellect has less value to them, or so I am told.

It makes sense that Unity ends up completing this series. A path of joy unfolds the effortlessness and simplicity of the journey home. The Way of Nothing destroys all concepts leaving nothing but what is. Finally we end up with the obviousness of Unity.

Unity is difficult without a Path of Joy, and impossible while we are holding onto concepts.

In the end Unity is a Path of Joy as both are inseparable from each other. To walk in Unity is to walk in joy, and the good news is you can begin in that joy right now without having to wait for a special event to happen in the future. Just don't take anything too seriously and burst.

I will prove it to you; just fake a smile right now as you are reading this, there you go, look around and make sure no one is going to judge you for being in joy. It's our secret agreement. If you need to, cover your mouth and smile for no reason but don't laugh because this is not funny, it is very serious; it is very profound stuff we are talking about. Welcome to a path of joy. Now we can continue and not be serious about enlightenment.

Throw away your robes, your books (not this one because you are reading it) and all your concepts but 'keep your shirt on'... we are not in a rush.

Seriousness can only take you so far. It can take you to the edge of the mind but instead of jumping it will analyze to death what is beyond. We can call this "beyond" or "death of separation" Unity. It is beyond because the mind cannot access it. All that is allowed to enter is what can fit through the eye of a needle.

Very few people end up fitting through this needle, and instead stay comfortable with what they believe they have and own. What we own physically, emotionally, mentally and spiritually ends up weighing us down so much that we cannot fly. This does not mean throwing away your house and car. Please don't throw away your kids or your parents to get enlightened; believe it or not they will actually help you to be free.

Yes, we have eaten too much cheesecake to fit through the needle, but I know how good cheesecake tastes. Unity, however, tastes even better. By continuing to surrender, the way is certain and fitting through is only a matter of grace.

Is Unity really the end, or is it beginning?

Whichever way you look at it, the end result is the same. In our tradition, we say Unity is the birthright of every human. It is this that is the beginning of capital 'L' life. In fact there is really no life without it.

Life has always been unified; it is our perceptions of life that are not. This book is for those who are not completely satisfied with these perceptions and intuit that there is more than meets the eye. You will not read so much about the path leading up to Unity, but more as to what Unity is currently. It is based on the view or lens of the author's approach to Unity. Of course we have established earlier that there is no author, but we can pretend.

Also, what happens after Unity? Is it a mystical experience? Is it reachable? What is it like to live in that? Are there still thoughts and feelings? What are the benefits and disadvantages to being an enlightened somebody? (More like a 'nobody'.)

It is my intention to try to answer these questions, talk about the obvious and some other stuff too.

Ironically Unity is sought after and perceived as a goal, when in fact it is simply a place to start from scratch, much like hitting a reset button on a computer. It is a fresh place to begin and is a clean slate without conditioning or programming. Don't worry, you don't have to do anything about your programming; just leave it alone for now and come along for the ride.

Many books have been written about this goal of enlightenment or freedom. I personally take what resonates and leave the rest. I encourage you to do the same with this material.

Have you ever reread a book or re-watched a movie after some time has passed and it was a completely new experience?

This is what it is like with the perception of Unity. Clarity is ongoing because Unity is a new aliveness and is ever revealing. It is fresh popcorn popping. Perception is just along for the ride giving us a way to express the inexpressible.

Unity can never actually be captured in its entirety and then distilled into a form. This is wonderful because it means it is much greater than all attempts to do so throughout the ages. All anyone can do is humbly (or not) share one's experience. In this sense anyone could write a book on Unity because everyone has a take or perception they can share even if that is "I don't know." Ironically I don't know is probably the greatest description of Unity, but we will get to that a bit later.

Depending on our perception at a given time, we could be drawn to one particular book. For whatever reason you have been drawn to this one right now, which tells me a lot about where you are at on the spiritual journey. There are no accidents.

This does not mean that you have achieved a certain level of knowledge so that you can understand what is written here. You do not need to understand a word here at all. It means you are more interested in the experiencing of Unity than picking up dry concepts. That being said, this material does indeed contain concepts throughout, but the underlying intention is to steer you away from them so you can see the obviousness that you are already free. Throughout our journey make a game of it; we are exploring the greatest mystery there is… what we are.

What I have observed is that usually Unity is described as an 'end result' and while it may be true that no one can understand it unless it is experienced, I believe there is no value in supporting the concept that it is an object to be attained. Instead I prefer to present it as it is now, an alive and current happening despite perceptions to the contrary.

The descriptions of Unity in the past or what could happen after Unity are only meant to provide insight into Unity as a whole that includes all of the parts. Since Unity is eternal understanding, what happens after Unity is the same as understanding what happens now and even before.

So what is the point in writing about Unity when the perception of it will change?

Even though perceptions will change, including my own, Unity will not. A perception is like a snapshot of Reality, the clearer the shot, the easier to see the whole picture. In this same way the universe puts together our very own slide show. At first the images may be blurry, but then through surrender they get clearer until all that remains is openness. This openness has no end or beginning. This is the Eternal Union with what you are. It is a wonderful story and hopefully this material here will play a small part in it. It is my attempt to add a "perception of Unity slide" into the mix.

If this slide helps in any way then great; if not, there are many other slides out there that I can recommend. *A Course in Miracles* (*ACIM*) also makes this point, even though it is arguably one of the clearest descriptions of Unity available. Now more than ever I understand why the 'author' does not make the book out to be 'the best'. It is because it would limit the infinite ways in which the invitation for oneness presents itself. The best is simply what works in the moment. The best could be a lump of coal – if it works, then super!

While I think *ACIM* is an amazing book it is not everyone's cup of Unity. Some people get bored just looking at it. I have enjoyed reading it before, but the thought of going through it again is not appealing at this point. That being said, I also know the value of the material and how useful it has been to millions of people. My father specifically benefited.

This work is not special, but like each work, its value is in its uniqueness. Unity is the same regardless of the uniqueness of expression. This uniqueness applies not just to books but individuals, music, art etc. I like this one because it was written through this expression of Paramananda. He is so cool, at least in my humble opinion.

I assure you that if you pick up a book on knitting, languages or photography, you would want the author to have expertise in those areas. For example if you bought a book on Spanish you would want the person to know how to speak it. Maybe you could get away with writing a beginner's Spanish book if you had been to Mexico on vacation a few times. "¿Quiero cerveza por favor?" or "¡Baño rápido!"

The tricky thing with this material is that even though you want the author to be an expert, if he actually believes he is then that disqualifies him as an expert in the subject. This is the danger of picking up a book like this because chances are the person writing it actually thinks they know what they are talking about. This in turn can lead the reader down some strange paths to say the least. I have been down some of them in the past myself and my attempt with this work is to save the reader some time by possibly avoiding some of those weird twists and turns.

Any authority is from Unity itself and not from an individual. Unfortunately this becomes difficult to discern as we traverse the path. Laughing at all this mumbo jumbo helps a lot, because you don't want any of it to stick to you. If you laugh hard enough, hopefully it will fall off. If it doesn't, just scrape it off and flick it onto the ground. Don't pick it up, because that's gross!

Of course at the same time, falling off track or going down those dark places is also part of the show, and possibly your path. No matter how well informed we may be, we sometimes slip. I would never wish to deny someone the chance of falling off the wagon or wandering off the beaten path. There is tremendous value in falling and failing. I have fallen off so many times I have lost count. Ouch. How else can we see the difference between peace and pain? My hope is that you have already done much of your falling and failing; the more the better.

I certainly would not take away any of those experiences, since they are at the very least a part of the story. They are a source of amusement for the 'Unity parties' the angels have for us. That being said there comes a point in every story when the character is ready for the whole enchilada of enlightenment. Are you at this point yet? If you are not, you can still read on and maybe be inspired to jump on later.

So I am not an expert, but a beginner who has some experience on the subject or rather on the subjectivity of Unity. I will share from this perspective, but I do not claim to know anything special or have something that you do not have right now this very instant.

I consider myself an explorer of Silence. My resume is not fancy; it is simple. I practice exploring eyes closed and eyes open. My attention and intention is to always rest in what is real and does not change.

No one is a Unity Master – Unity masters you.

Unity is a result of resonance with the Silence. While I cannot give credit to an actual 'person' for giving it to 'me', the fact remains that I surrender everything to the Teacher as the Silence.

While hypothetically Unity could happen at any moment for anyone, that is not my experience. I needed a physically living teacher that knew me so well as to see into my heart, mind and ego with burning bright high beams. I was a slippery sucker I guess.

I was willing and currently am willing to do what it takes to be free. This did not take the difficulties out of the path, but made and makes Unity inevitable since there then becomes no other option. Like my Teacher said to a group of us once, "Close the back door."

The Teacher never stops shining the Light because they are the light. The Teacher is the Silence pointing to the Silence, which is already free within all humans, and maybe even frogs too.

That being said I am open to the possibility that it may be different for you or anyone else. There are those who say you cannot be enlightened by reading a book, but have they read this one? So fingers crossed and good luck!

I will attempt to be completely honest and frank and in a sense come out of the closet with the subject! I will hold nothing back from you.

To clarify when I use the terms "you" and "me" understand that in the experience of Unity there is no separate individual. No one becomes 'Unified' or 'Enlightened' because these are simply labels for the absence of being a separate individual.

It is like everyone carries around two 'you's' or a You-you: One is separate and the underlying one is silent. I am talking to the silent one.

The danger for the seeker is in believing they will get something for themselves in Unity. I say danger in the sense that the seeker is a product of time and thinking. In this way seeking increases time and therefore the separation is prolonged in some cases.

This is why I wrote *The Way of Nothing* to assist in destroying that idea. It takes a certain ripeness of maturity to understand that. I am not trying to be condescending here, but simply honest. This point is a time saver if you get it. I would not be sharing this with you if I did not chase Unity as an object for what seemed an eternity. I was very one-pointed and serious about getting it which is why it got further away.

I will not spend too much time trying to destroy concepts here but instead try to give you something to resonate with. Regardless of how you feel, I hope in some way I can help to demystify the 'experience' so that perhaps at the very least a few bumps might be avoided. If you are to hit them, however, there is nothing anyone can do to stop you from hitting them.

Don't forget to ask for help if you get stuck!

In the end, I have nothing for you!

I have no idea what this 'holding nothing' will look like, but let's strap on our 'Advanced' Unity helmets and find out.

You Knit Tea

What is the difference between You Knit Tea and Unity? At first the difference may seem clear. The mind looks at You Knit Tea and the words are immediately dismissed as incoherent nonsense; but at the same time, something might be resonating with the sound it forms. It sounds exactly like Unity, but it is in a different form than what we have been taught to accept as true. This Unity seems hidden from us even though the vibration of the word is exactly the same when we sound it out. There is no difference.

This is the essence of the challenge in describing that which is both obvious and secret. It depends on the perception of the mind as it filters, categorizes and judges. The mind is constantly filtering out what it thinks is important for the separate individual. Unity is beyond that process of separation, and can only be known as it is without the mental conceptions that continue to bombard the simplicity of that seeing which is already happening.

It only takes an instant to see; we do not need to wait for the mind to stop thinking permanently; that would be impossible and fortunately for us it is also unnecessary. The mind does a good job at what it does. It is supposed to think. We simply need to see this process of thinking for what it is so that we can discern truth.

It would be true to say, reality is the exact opposite of our notions because it is notion-less. This is why it is difficult to convey in words, but this does not mean we cannot have a little fun trying to get the penny to drop.

In the English language when you break apart a word into syllables the word loses its meaning. For example the sounds 'EL', 'LA' and 'FANT' do not mean anything on their own yet when you put them together they form elephant. Each syllable has no essential meaning on its own.

Now it sounds like I am on *Sesame Street*. El La Fant... Elephant.

Not all languages are like this, however. In the Sanskrit language, each syllable has both a meaning and a vibrational significance that represents the syllable that forms the word. This means that the whole word is literally the combination of the meanings of each syllable. The vibration of Sanskrit is said to be very close to being the vibration of what something actually is in essence.

Everything is a vibration of energy (except for no-thing); and like magic, certain words come close to vibrating at the same frequency as what they attempt to describe.

If you take a look at Paramananda: 'Pa' 'Ra' 'Ma' 'nan' 'da'. Each syllable has meaning to form the whole vibration of the word. As you put them together they also form meaning. 'Para' is Heaven, highest or supreme. 'Parama' is the Supreme or divine mother. 'Ananda' is Peace, Love and Joy. Therefore you get the highest bliss of the divine mother. Paramananda is a strange enough name. Can you imagine introducing yourself as the supreme heavenly Bliss of the Divine Mother? That sounds a little pretentious don't you think! This is why I go by P instead.

The names we are given at birth seldom do justice or provide any clues as to what the name is supposed to represent. For example Bob does not really tell us about the essence of what Bob is beyond what is on the label. Aside from the surface appearance, he is actually the most loving and tender man you could ever meet. When in his presence you feel accepted and you can be comfortable in your own skin. The vibration of Bob could be called 'Sukra' in Sanskrit, which is the God of Love. This would be a more accurate representation or label of Bob's essence.

The Sanskrit name describes the essence or vibration of the spirit as it is happening in manifestation. This is why some monks or sages you might have heard of have Sanskrit names, even if they are not born into that culture. If correctly cognized the name more accurately represent this essence.

What the name stands for is the potential flow of vibration or how the spirit can be appearing to the world. In this sense everyone in the world has a Sanskrit name that represents his or her essence. Don't ask me yours because I don't know how to figure that one out. The ancient Rishis (sages) could somehow see this essence and discern an accurate label.

This was important in the old days. Imagine if you were having an arranged marriage based on the label and your partner had been mislabeled. Your husband could be totally inappropriate when you unwrapped him on your wedding day. You could end up marrying an elephant (Ganesh) instead of a monkey (Hanuman). And you bought all those bananas for no reason!

Usually we never live up to what this essence represents, and instead are just living life as Bob or Rick. There is nothing wrong with being Rick or Bob, yet obviously there is much more behind the label in every case. Whether the label is a clear representation or not it is still only a pointer.

The Infinite expresses in infinite divine uniquenesses that are all transcendent of the individual ego. Therefore what Bob is is way bigger than he can comprehend. He is Sukra, the God of Love.

In Unity, without there being any labels, that which is of the highest expression is left to shine through the individual. Nothing is required for Bob to do; yet if Bob dissolves into the Silence through a practice, the essence of what is becomes more obvious to him. In other words when Bob loses himself (or his 'self' – the part that feels separate) what is left is a more accurate expression of the infinite.

Of course his friends still call him Bob because it would be weird to do otherwise, but Bob becomes less identified with the

Character. Now the relationship with the world shifts as he has seen through the past programming. This is seeing with new eyes or the cosmic eye.

Bob does not shift his attention or identify with another character but simply rests in the Silence without labels. By practicing Silence and allowing everything gets clearer.

The point is that words or names seldom even come close to the vibration or essence of what something is even if they appear accurate. They are used as convenience only in today's world. It was not always like this, however.

The sacredness of vibration was honored in order to preserve the integrity of Unity. This is a lost art that perhaps would have helped us to remember that ancient root of all vibrations... The Silence.

Now the only way to reconnect with that art of seeing what 'IS' is to go to the root. There is no other way than finding out the source of all vibrational energy.

It does not matter whether you call me Rick, Paramananda, P or Princess. They are all just labels for what is indescribable or a mystery. I will tell you one is a more accurate vibrational description than the others and NO it is not Princess!!!!

I am not saying that 'I am' Paramananda, however, because that is not true either. What I am saying is that Paramananda is a more accurate label of the highest potential of what remains when all is surrendered into the Silence. It is a nice label.

You Knit Tea is only a label for the indescribable. We can call it 'gazzisherbob' or 'OM', but it is vibration-less. It is the root of all vibration. Whether you call it 'youknitea' or take it apart to 'you knit tea' it is the same. It is the underlying thing that cannot be accurately described by English or Sanskrit.

In truth Unity is always the reality behind the vibrations like You Knit Tea. These vibrations come together to shape the world of language and our interpretation of it.

Ultimately all labels are abandoned for Unity and then with

that clarity we can see what is happening effortlessly from this fresh innocent view.

These expressions of aliveness happen within Unity and are not separate from it.

Unity... What is This?

Would you be terribly disgusted with me if I said, "I don't know?"

And... the book goes in the garbage.

How can you describe that which is the most obvious in a clear and simple way?

It's here? Nowhere? This? That? Reality? Everywhere?

As you can see this does little to explain what it is to the intellect. At best all the intellect can do is form an idea around what these words represent. This is why in the clearest spiritual traditions the value is not in talking, discussing or analyzing but in tasting Unity. Tasting... 'the what' becomes experientially answered through undergoing what it is, as it is. To 'know' what a pear is, we taste it. The pear can be green or red but at some point reading about it does not do it justice. The question should be how can I taste the pear of Unity? It's all about the Zen of How!

In fact, ultimately it is not necessary to know what it is. Knowing or understanding is already inherent in the aliveness of the tasting. Everything else is only to satisfy the intellect, which is part of the story of awakening.

When clarity is unraveling for the student it is usually the result of some meditation and wisdom based on direct experience. (Meditation can be formal or otherwise; in a way everyone is meditating right now – the question becomes what are you meditating on?) The wisdom comes from experiencing what is not true more than understanding profound states of being. What is not Unity is easier to see than Unity. The mind is full of what we are not and to see this is to begin to see through its falseness. Seeing these covers one by one uncovers the obviousness of what we are. Neti neti, or, not this, not this.

So how can you describe the indescribable?

This is just it, nobody knows Unity as something tangible found in the head. The beauty of Unity is that it cannot be known in this heady intellectual way. It is this that makes it an unending and unfolding mystery of intuitive knowingness. This is knowingness without a knower.

It is an interpreting of the Silence that is for you to experience directly. Nobody can ever give it to you as an object. It is the Aliveness of all that is. It is the Teacher seeing what is. It is you in your essential nature without a separation.

Of course it has been expressed intentionally through every possible medium. Here we have the basis for every beautiful work of art. Here the artist is describing the indescribable oneness of all that is. It is felt in the core of our being and yet words fall short to capture it. It could even be expressed by staring into a child's eyes or into the eyes of your cat. It is a wonderful thing to attempt to describe through poetry, music, and painting, or as the Buddha did by staring at a flower for hours on end.

If we take notice of life with innocence we will see Unity everywhere. This is inevitable as we open up to the possibility that we have no real idea about what we are; we simply do not know. This is not tragic! It is liberating because the possibilities are now open. This innocent willingness to face the unknown is the joy of seeing what is already plain and simple. This is you right now, without lifting a finger; being fully and completely all there is.

The truth is that from this Unity as it is, everything is its description and expression. This is the wonder of being in Unity. This is sharing the same is-ness with all there is in existence. The world is an art gallery filled with every possible form imaginable.

Unity is seeing that the separation into human beings with different consciousnesses (most importantly your consciousness) is conceptual. There is only consciousness with the appearance of many minds that take ownership of the puppet-body.

The difficulty is that whatever is said can be grabbed by the mind as a concept. Even the most wonderful ideas are simply ideas, yet they can be powerful symbols that capture our attention to become 'my' truth. This is the dance that happens on the way to Unity. The dance is between the Silence of Nothingness and the shift of attention onto things that change and move.

The bottom line is that the mind wants to own Unity. At first it says quietly, "What is it?" Then the mind gets louder, "WHAT IS IT?"

Stop and Listen. "There sure are a lot of things not to think about."

Even the word Unity implies a process of unification in order to unify something into something else.

The Self is already unified with everything. What you are is already Unity. This is so because – taken to the extreme – a separate individual is only happening in Unity. From Unity there is only seeing or not seeing. When Unity happens and we become liberated (permanently) we are simply seeing for the first time. This is the insight of seeing that all there ever is is seeing. The not seeing part is only a dance happening within the seeing-ness of all there is. To see this obviousness is part of the adventure. The attitude of play is the best for moving into the insight (In Sight) of Unity.

This new seeing is hard to describe because it is eternal. Words and ideas more accurately describe 'things' happening in time and space. This is where we fall short again. Yet to under-stand this limitation is key and can bring us closer to seeing the futility of trying to figure it out. Understanding this point is very useful and relieving for the seeker. We cannot understand it. 'I don't know' is absolutely okay.

This is the wonderful beauty of Unity! Can you imagine if

Unity was understandable? If it was in the realm of knowledge we would all be in Unity. It would be taught in school and you could study to do it correctly. In the bookstore you could go pick up a book called Unity for Dummies. (I think there is an actual book called *Enlightenment for Dummies*.)

Imagine for a moment that for your whole life you have been asleep. Even right up to reading these words you are asleep. Then suddenly out of nowhere you wake up out of this sleep and can see that all you had ever thought about – what you are – was just a changing idea.

More than this, your awareness is crystal clear that you are in eternity. You see that you have always been free – or rather – there is only freedom. You are in awe of the fact that suffering seemed to happen to you your whole life.

You see that suffering had never happened. You don't see this as an idea; but that literally, suffering has never happened. What now brings you to tears of Joy is that you see that nobody in the history of humanity, including all of your friends and loved ones in all of time and space, has ever suffered. Now you see everyone is Free; again this is not an idea but what you are experiencing right now in Unity.

So you go walking outside to meet your friends. Sara walks up to you and says, "You are not going to believe what happened to me at lunch." She starts complaining about the service she received, saying all sorts of nasty things about the waitress.

Now you are truly in awe! Sara right now thinks she is separate from Unity. Why does she not see it? It is obvious there is only the oneness of everything. What can you say to Sara? Do you shake her or tell her she is free? Who cares about your service at lunch? Do you not see the absolute wonder of this magnificence happening?

As Sara is talking, it becomes more and more clear she does not know she is a Goddess. As she goes on complaining about the past, you have a hard time focusing on the story as it seems to take a huge amount of effort. Instead you watch her lips move and her eyebrows frown, and marvel at the Silence that is holding the capacity for Sara-ness to complain and believe she is separate. Sara is infinite Peace and unending Bliss.

What can you say to her? You say nothing because you have no idea where to begin.

Then after what seems like an eternity you hear a loud, "Well! Hello? Are you even listening to me? Isn't she rude?"

Then you search inside for something profound to say but all that comes from this infinite sea of Love is, "Yeah, she sounds rude!" It surprises you, as it comes out; why didn't you say anything profound?

To realize what Unity is is somewhat like discovering the space in which objects exist. We never pay attention to the space in which objects appear; yet here it is as the capacity for objects. To try to convince someone to put attention on the space instead of the objects sounds crazy. Why would you do that? Why would we put attention on the obvious?

As long as attention is on the objects we don't notice the obvious capacity. Of course this is just an analogy; walking around trying to focus on the space instead of objects and you might bump into a wall. Nonetheless, there it is already.

As long as there is a separate individual (as an object) we don't notice Unity (Capacity). Unity is the capacity or potential for everything happening.

As long as there appears to be a 'you' that is a separate individual, Unity is not seen. Yet this separation vanishes all the time because it has no solid foundation. To understand the illusory nature of separation through the direct experience of Silence reveals the obviousness of what is.

The Unity of what is, simply, is what remains throughout all of this exploration. It is always here, yes, but to taste this is what we truly want. What we want is the seeing-ness of all there is. It is already happening like this. You are already free because all there is is happening within this obviousness, including the appearance of being a separate individual. To seem separate sucks, yet this suck-ness is also in Unity!

It does not matter how long you believe you are separate. It could have been millions of years, but that changes nothing. But to you, the one reading these words, it does matter. It matters because separation, while being a temporary phenomenon (millions of years is still temporary), still sucks while it is an experience. It feels real, does it not? There is no denying the reality of that even if we say it is apparent.

It is of little comfort to understand concepts because eventually we have to face the self on this path to Unity. It can seem like there are a tremendous number of obstacles to move before we can get up to the top of the mountain. It seems like there is so much we have to do to prepare.

We have to be still, allow, and not take anything seriously. To simplify, just pick one and relax.

How do we get ready for Unity?

Make it a priority and everything will happen on its own. This includes any preparation such as forgiving your mother or healing your past life karma. The only reason we become aware of any thought or feeling is to let it go. It will keep coming up until there is no resistance to it. Some of these patterns go on unnoticed which is a given; over time we see the show and therefore the distance between the patterns becomes wider.

Walking the walk is simply allowing everything as it comes without resistance. In fact allowing resistance as well if it comes up is the path. This is a path of Joy. You are already on the path. You have no control over what you 'get' on this path in each moment. The important point is to understand that whatever comes is only for you to let go of.

What is happening right now as you breathe and see these words is your path; everything that happens is your path. It is your path to Unity because this, right here, is the opportunity to see the obvious.

The forms and textures this path will take are unique to you. What comes up for YOU will be based on your past programming and what God decides to trick you with. (In a nice way, hopefully.) What comes up is very special to you as a separate person, which is why it seems so personal and real. It is all about 'you' waking up, or so it seems in the story.

Simultaneous to this appearance of being separate is a path of Joy. By exploring the Silence and discovering what it is to hold nothing, the obvious can POP up.

This is YOUR discovery and only you can tell me what Unity is because I have no clue. So what you need to do is find out and tell me based on your own discovery.

Expect that you will get it wrong because you will! This is exciting news because Unity is beyond what you come up with. You will never get it, but most certainly you will be it since you already are it.

Remember: Don't expect me to have the answers; I am just an explorer like you. Let's keep exploring together and see what we come up with.

In Sight

How can you see the obviousness of the fact that what is seeing is insight? In Unity there is no separation from insight, they are one and the same.

What are you seeing from?

Everything you need to see (not with the eyes but with insight) you are already seeing in Unity. Nothing is hidden. Seeing this is Unity.

Who is it that has something missing from their divine sight?

Insight is already happening now. Seeing is current – not something arising in the future. It is the re-recognition of this fact that this is the goal of spirituality. Our Being is not missing anything from this view because it is the entire view itself. What we are is this totality of wisdom that cannot be acquired. This is wonderful news for anyone who can't seem to get enough wisdom.

I am not saying it is bad to learn things and study. (I still go to school once in a while.) Even reading about Unity you might learn a thing or two (hopefully that you have no clue about anything at all). When seen in the clear light of Being, learning is a tool or even a kind of hobby. Some people are just interested in certain topics, like fishing, or law or nothingness. Preferences are a part of our character.

When it comes to the spiritual quest, however, certain people can become obsessed with gaining wisdom, which is like adding spiritual dust particles to your already-clean glasses.

The problem is that the separate individual does not see that the insight they seek is already happening. Insight is something he or she feels they need to get in order for the pieces of the puzzle to fall into place. The only step or piece that can be missing is the awareness of Silence. There is no other step to insight or Unity other than this.

Insight is not another object to be attained, but is the spontaneous recognition that there is only Unity. This is seeing.

From this perspective we can still put together the puzzle, but out of the sheer joy of doing a puzzle, not for what we will see in the end. Just look on the box the puzzle comes in. There it is, there is the picture. Now what?

Simply have fun exploring.

You are not the separate individual that seems to be missing something. This does not mean to deny being you and all that you appear to be, however. Yes, you have a sense of self. So What? Who doesn't? The point is that you are not a separate self. Being separate is what seems to make the difference. To try to change yourself in any way is pointless and only can aggravate the problem of 'the search'. A path of Joy is not about changing you, but about seeing what is already happening. The insight allows you to see the truth of what is happening even now as you read these words in your head.

What can happen in moments is that you melt into the Silence and allow all that is to shine. Do you need to flip a switch in your head for this to happen?

You need do so little in this process because allowing is our natural way of being anyway. Allowing is already happening effortlessly from being what you are. This insight is a natural function of consciousness exploring the absolute. It is playing a game of discovery to prove its existence to itself. Learning to have fun within the game makes all the difference. Then the puzzle puts itself together before your cosmic eye. Now you can see the picture and not just a memory of what was on the box.

Whether or not the sense of self is there is irrelevant in this playing. It is simply a function of what is happening and ironically this 'you' center has nothing to do with the BIG you. The process of playing can be effortless with a little insight.

The funny thing about this whole enlightenment thing is that it would be unnecessary if we were just okay with ourselves. This is impossible for the spiritual seeker, because it seeks what it thinks it is missing. The irony is that if we were content with our self in ignorance there would be no problem; we simply would go about our day. This is 'ignorance is bliss' in full operation. I used to think, "Everyone else is so lucky, because they don't care about enlightenment." They worry about money, or relationships. We get to worry about that plus being spiritual. I know that it sucks to have one more thing to worry about, but I didn't make up the rules.

I remember very clearly, wishing I could go back and forget about all this spiritual crap. Insight, enlightenment and meditation, who needs all of this? Throw it away because it just seems to hurt. I want to go back to the good old days when all I was thinking about was my next hamburger and Coke. (I still think like this... nothing and snacks... mmmm... snacks – that's how my brain functions.)

This is the problem with being the chosen one. Once you have been bitten by Unity, there is no choice but to go for it. The sooner we get over this limbo between ignorance and knowledge, separation and freedom, the better. So let's bring it on and get over it quickly so we can get back to enjoying the burger. (A veggie burger if you are Vegan.)

The Zen of Unity

Unity is the ZEN of being this. (This meaning, what is real right now.) This is waking up with fresh eyes in every moment, and living without holding onto what comes naturally. ZEN is the exploration of nothingness that is both infinite treasure and nothing at all. It is absolute emptiness without a concept of what emptiness is. It is absolute fullness without a concept of what fullness is. This fullness/emptiness becomes the obvious Zen of Unity.

What can be done to live in this ZEN WOW?

In Unity there is only this ZEN. WOW! This makes it easy because there really is no other choice. At least from Unity there is no other intelligent choice. Joy is so much more delicious than pain, is it not? This is how easy the choice becomes. It becomes a 'no choice' because it is obvious that any other choice but staying in ZEN is ridiculously silly.

Why would you consciously choose to stick your tongue on a frozen pole in -40 degree weather? Well, yes I did that once, but I will never do it again.

Why would anyone in their sanity choose something other than all there is? This is how the dream came about in the first place. Consciousness put attention on something other than what it is. Maybe it did this to prove its existence. Maybe it chose this by accident. Oooooops! This is the cosmic, "Ooooops, I did it again."

This apparent something (separate subject) that we think we are seems to make the choice. This separate subject is only a belief that it is the center of operations. This is the tiny 'me' center talking.

At this point let's not point fingers except in the direction of Unity. Of course, what is pointing the finger and the finger itself is the ZEN of Unity.

What is ZEN?

Zen is Unity.

Even Buddha never knew that. (He never knew that because there is only Zen without a Knower or a pretend subject.) Buddha didn't know anything.

I know everyone says he did but that is because they are all wrong. If you don't believe me ask him for yourself.

I told you... nothing but Zen.

Inspiration

You don't have to look very far if what you are is already the inspiration you look for. This is the simplicity of divine inspiration. Seeing this elsewhere is only a side effect of being what you are already.

Have you ever really got excited when you understood something you were trying to figure out?

Imagine that inspiration is like a constant answer and a constant mystery at the same time. Boredom cannot exist since all there is is this wonderful engagement with LIFE. Life is an inspiration because it is a mystery to the mind. Life is an inspiration because it is alive with potential.

What is the purpose or meaning of life? Why am I here? What am I? Is there a God? (Insert your own questions here.)

Many people struggle to answer these deep questions and I have observed that some even believe they have the answers. Maybe you are one of them. There is nothing wrong with knowing your purpose or finding out why I am here – at least I don't think there is.

I used to think that I had to find these things out to be happy. In fact I would have bet my life that I was unhappy because I didn't have those answers.

I was very broken and incomplete until I knew my purpose. So I took special courses to break down the walls so I could see it. On one of those courses, out of thirty or so people I think I was the one who said, "I don't know." I had failed… so I did the only thing I could think to pass this highly important course… I lied.

I told everyone that my purpose was to share bliss with the world. Everyone thought that was great and that it suited me (I even believed it) so they cheered me on. I thought that maybe this was my purpose, maybe I had found it. Finally after all the searching I had one answer of what I was to do. But how was I to do that? How do you share Bliss with the world?

It is easy to come up with an answer mentally to these questions, but what we want is to dissolve the questioner and be the answer. Who cares what the answer actually is! As long as the answer is what is alive and real, does it really matter?

The problem comes with the expectation of what we think life should look like based on our ideas, concepts, options, conditionings etc. I thought something was wrong with me because I could not find the answer mentally. The truth is, I still don't have the answer in this conceptual way.

After the taking the purpose course, I was mentally and emotional inspired, but that inspiration provided by the group energy and cheering did not last more than a couple of days and then it was gone. Did I forget my purpose? How can I keep the inspiration alive to live my purpose?

You exist. Isn't that amazing! Here you are. Aren't you the luckiest person in the whole world!

In the Silence, when there was nothing to hold onto, I had to face the honesty of 'I don't know'. A purpose, a meaning to my life or my 'divine mission' had become just a nice thought to entertain my spiritual ego. Now I could hold onto this special purpose, but to do that would be superficial, at least in my case. The truth was it was so painful and took so much effort to think about this idea that I gave it up. I said to God, "Look if you want me to do anything specific then you'd better do it because I am not going to."

Often we become too glamorized by the spiritual purpose to see the obvious staring at us. We miss all the steps because we are lost in the future. Right now your purpose is to be reading these words. This is not an assumption but a fact; otherwise you would not be reading them. This is divine simplicity. For the spiritual ego, however, this is not a 'good enough' purpose. "Hell no! You need to be doing something much greater for yourself and humanity other than just reading."

There is nothing wrong with an idea or moving towards a purpose and goal (even Unity), but honesty is also important. Is the idea or concept more important than tasting Unity? If Unity is your purpose then your purpose should be to forget all of this and simply relax. If you are going to put your mind on anything other than Silence, put it on the Zen of How. But how?

In the end the only conclusion or answer is to make the Silence within the most important thing to focus on. No matter what is happening, the stillness of Unity is the only true inspiration. It is dismissed as too normal and certainly does not have a big flashy sign saying, "Look, I am good enough!"

The more attention that I gave to the Silence, the more I felt I was living on purpose. None of this requires thought or conceptualization; there is nothing to figure out. I would think that many have gone to their deaths without feeling as though they came here to do what they were supposed to. In a way they were right, because what if the very thing that would give a sense of purpose was to just 'shut up' and be quiet.

In the Silence, inspiration is constant; you need look nowhere else than the unchanging-ness for your special purpose. You won't actually find it because YOU ARE IT! This is the whole irony of searching for inspiration on the outside. Yes it does point inwards sometimes but the true inspiration is in Unity with all that is.

The other irony is that the less you think about it, the more you actually live it. This is the idea of living on purpose. You already are the gift for the world. Just be you, exactly as you are with all your silliness and so-called flaws. Be inspired by the source and what happens next is magic. This is the popcorn effect in full peppiness and Popping-ness.

Before you know it, you are living a higher purpose because the essence of what is uniquely expressing has nothing in the way. The idea is to surrender to a higher will.

Even the most inspired sages, scientists or philosophers with all their combined wisdom only saw a piece of the pie. They saw a concept or idea or if they were lucky they saw nothingness. This is not a failure but a wonderful sign from infinity. This says that that inspiration itself is an eternal dance. This is aliveness that always is revealing more and more of the pie. The pie is huge, infinite in fact, and just when we think we cannot handle the vastness of infinity it gives us more to be inspired about. This is a free gift, like staring into the facelessness of God.

Who cares about what you need to do to feel fulfillment when your very nature is fulfillment itself. This is the inward dance of exploration.

Like rays coming off of the Sun, there is no end. One ray will enlighten and move us into inner wonder, yet there is another and another. There is no time to see the full beauty which is why we have eternity to see it. This is not an eternity of time but an eternity of this-here-and-now. This seeing only happens in Eternity. Time is not even outside of eternity because nothing is outside of eternity, at least from the perspective of Unity.

There is no space to adequately fill the glory of God. Even the Universe is not big enough. So we create infinite universes. Yet that is not enough, so we end up in an infinite inspiration of mystery. This is why you have had millions of lives. Not so you could wake up but because you love it. You love the drama of being a separate character. Now you love the drama of trying to wake up. Nothing I can do can stop you or get you to wake up because it is all your doing as the eternal being yourself. It is your fault! If you are tired of coming back to earth then wake up, stop reincarnating and get a life. Find something else to inspire you in some other higher spiritual dimension.

The most beautiful scenery in nature that inspires awe is only at the periphery of the awe of this Silence. The beauty is within. This is no understatement. In Unity, all that exists exists to reveal its innate beauty as it is. The forms in creation are only the perfect expression of what wears them. This is only the very tip of the iceberg of inspiration.

The forms are only an attempt of the infinite artisan to display the magnificence of what is.

Intuition

Intuition is a term that is also misunderstood. When I used to think of intuition I would think of something psychic happening like seeing into the future. Later on I understood it to mean knowingness, like a gut feeling. Often this is called women's intuition. Like other guys, I would shy away from this since we men are too macho for that. Intuition includes but is much bigger than these ideas. We could call this bigger intuition or 'ultimate sense' a Uni-intuition.

In the Silence without movement, the universe is constantly giving us opportunities to see into the heart of reality. Where we go and what we do is an intuitive dance with no effort. There is no need to ponder the next move on the dance floor because before we even know it we are dancing the next move. Even if that move is stumbling with awkwardness it is a divinely guided awkward stumbling. Intuition is what is sliding our feet around without us having the chance think about it.

In daily life most of the world is not consciously aware of the connection to this flow of Silence. Whenever this intuition does appear to happen, it is seen as miraculous. It is miraculous, but what makes it even more magical is that it is always present; we simply are staring in another direction.

Without conceptualizing what does uni-intuition mean?

It is how everything is happening right now on planet earth and even way out on the other side of the universe. There is no end to this happening.

Unity is intuitively known. Everyone has a sense of Unity that they can tap into in moments of beauty, meditation, and prayer or even 'accidentally' during shocking events like bungee jumping. Of course this intuition is not actual stabilized Unity, but it is a movement or step towards the glimpse. This is what *ACIM* refers to as "the holy instant". It seems divided in time, but stretch out this intuition and the eternal nature is seen in its holy instant.

As children we lived in this Intuition. We felt connected to the world, nature, rocks, people, bees, ants etc.

Intuition gets more and more refined as one moves along a path of Joy. Ultimately, Unity and intuition merge into a uni-intuitive awareness of oneness. This happens when the person who owns the intuition starts to dissolve into the Silence. At this point instead of being directed by a phantom outside force, there is only intuition moving the puppet 'body/mind' in each instant.

It is difficult for the separate individual to understand this because it can't imagine life without being in control. All the while and without conscious awareness, this intuition has been directing life through the filter of separation. The separate individual has no idea of how little control it has ever had. The idea of being in charge and isolated was only for the benefit of the ego. To see the total lack of control in one instant would be terrifying to this little self. This is evidence of the Love of God that we are being shown in only glimpses and not the whole shebang all at once. This is like stepping into a pool, first your toe, then your foot. Slowly you go in and then with a little cosmic oomph you dive in. Then it's all fun and games until someone loses an ego.

Scientists are currently making breakthroughs into this illusion of control. Life indeed happens more magically than we ever could conceive.

Intuition is the Divine Grace and Holy Spirit that does not move you as a separate piece but is the big you moving. This is intuitively known, deep in the heart. We long to unite with this free flowing guidance that automatically knows the next step to take or thing to say. If you take an honest look at all the steps in your life, it will become clear that a separate 'you' had very little to do with getting 'you' to the point of reading these words right now. It had nothing to do with this separate 'you'. It was not personal. You would not want to be in charge anyway, that would be a guaranteed disaster. The bottom line is that the universe just lets you think you are tying your shoelaces and running the multimillion-dollar corporation.

The personal part happening was part of the great story of you. It is your own DVD that is labeled with your name on it. It has on it all the things you wanted to do but couldn't in the deleted scenes section. It is not personal because it is just a story being played. The stop button is broken on the remote, only the pause functions sometimes in emergencies.

Uni-intuition sees through this story.

In Unity there is no outside agent guiding since there is only the Divine; therefore each step or word said is Divine. This is difficult to understand and I would say use your intuition if you are going to attempt to understand it at all. The difficulty and problem is only for the separate individual, not for the intuition of Unity.

Having to direct and guide life as a separate individual is not natural, but good on us for trying so hard to do it anyway. You get a gold star for that one for sure! I think one day we should get medals for trying to live our lives on our own. It still amazes me that people actually believe they are living and running their own show. Of course the problem is that then they are responsible for what happens in them. This responsibility is only a belief that the world is on their shoulders and that they really can make a difference on their own.

How many events did you really have control of in your life? Think about it!

I admire those who seem to have it together, but I admire the most those who have fallen apart and seem to have lost it all. That inspires me because it opens them up to a new possibility.

The new possibility of seeing can be the magical moment that frees up life from the chains of limitation.

These people are very open to something much greater than what this little self created. Even dirt can inspire them.

How can dirt inspire those who have lost it all? I actually met someone who got inspired by dirt. His name was David and he was on the top of the world (at least financially). Then he lost it all. He lost his money, his house, his 'friends', but more importantly he lost his arrogance and his control. Starting over and left with nothing, he began to see the magic of simply living.

It is the magic of starting over and seeing with the new eyes of intuition that opens inspiration. You decide to create a garden but have no dirt. Then you see your neighbor has a huge pile of dirt that she can't wait to get rid of. She offers it to you and you are in dirt heaven. It is that simple; now you can plant your carrots.

It is the little miracles of life that are missed while we are trying to run around making things work better. It works just like John Lennon said, "Life is what happens while you're busy making other plans."

While we are thinking and imagining that we are in control, life happens. The results are not in your control. Anyone who takes a moment to think about this will see its obviousness. If it is seen without conceptualizing, the surrendering of control is very simple and a matter of ordinary common sense. No offense intended to those who don't surrender, but what are you doing? Are you loco?

Of course the question is how can I surrender if I have no idea what I am surrendering to?

EXACTLY! This is the most important point in the book. Finding out what this 'Silence' or 'Stillness' is that is mentioned over and over in different ways as your true self is STEP ONE. It is also all the steps after. Unity is simple after step one. Unity is impossible without step one.

Surrendering into that, the step disappears and there is only oneness. In that oneness the intuition takes over all the steps. In Unity there is guidance from the Unknown. The separate individual would think that divine intuition is the knowing of things from one moment to the next. It gets excited at the idea of knowledge because it gives a sense of being in control of its life. Therefore the expression "knowledge is power".

Of course you can see the trap; if this is the limited intuition you want then this will be 'you' being more in charge with more knowledge, which is not Unity.

True intuition happens when 'you' stop knowing. It seems backwards and it is. You could say that intuitive knowing is a type of intuition, but that happens for a highly advanced separate individual only.

Intuitive unknowing happens in Unity without a separate individual. The appearance of 'knowing' is only an appearance. The wisdom of intuition is having no special knowledge. Anything that happens for the uni-intuitive is automatic and is unknowable and un-own-able. This is intuition in the purest and most refined sense available for the human.

How do we get this cosmic super advanced refined automatic razor sharp intuition?

It's already there – just stop thinking so much!

Revelation

The revelation is not 'out there' or even 'in here' but this (what is happening right now). This is the revelation. I don't mean these words here, but everything that is happening right now. This revelation is current and ongoing. It is seeing into the wonder that this is all there is. By "this" I mean Silence, stillness, breathing, reading, feeling, seeing, stretching, scratching or whatever is going on.

I know revelation sounds a bit biblical but that is not my fault. I use it because it implies 'to reveal'. If you want, I could change it to 'reveal-ation' because revelation is actually about revealing what is eternal. Since we are being picky about words, it is interesting to note that the 'revel' of revelation means to 'take pleasure' or 'delight in'. This is certainly an applicable definition because the revelation is the delight or joy of the infinite revealing itself.

A Path of Joy is the Joy of exploring the Silence, which reveals all there is. All there is is THIS.
Unity can be described as the act of reveling in the revealing or in other words enjoying the unfolding mystery of self-exploration.

There is no 'Book of Revelations' out there. All great spiritual books are merely pointing out tiny snapshots of the greater picture of revelation as it is happening currently.

In Unity everything becomes revelatory including the most mundane of activities. Actually it is not the activity itself but the aliveness in which it is happening that is freshly revealing. Picking your nose is gross, but that is also part of revelation in Unity. It is truly divine because there is no picker, picking is happening within ALL THERE IS. Still, just because it is divine does not mean that you should do it public. And no I am not trying to be picky here. (Sorry, I lost control again.)

This never stops being revelatory because it is always Alive and fresh. It is the opposite of the dry and boring-ness of thinking (as a separate individual). Thoughts, stories and concepts can only appear to be satisfying to a person who has not disappeared into the Silence. (At this point I want to clear up the assumption that there are not thoughts, stories or thinking happening in Unity. Anything is possible in Unity, thinking can and does happen, but as a natural function of intuition, not separation. For example, thinking happens when it is useful: learning at school, figuring out a technical solution at work. This type of intuitive thinking does not require a separate thinker, but is only a natural function of what is happening. This is 'impersonal' thinking.)

How do you disappear into the Silence? Through reveling in it... yum yum!

Once the Silence has been seen as valuable (that the Silence is valuable is an understatement), the revelation begins.

This is delightful!

Para

Para is a Sanskrit word that means the self, supreme or heaven. We are living in Para right now simultaneous to our so-called 'regular lives'. In these lives, our heaven sense or 'Para sense' has become dull due to lack of use or attention. This has come about through the avoidance of the Silence. The sweetness of Para has become unfamiliar because our senses are unrefined enough to allow the light in. Too many doughnuts, I guess.

Seriously though, I am not just talking about what we eat or smoke but what we focus on. Our attention is not on heaven therefore the senses have stopped revealing our world correctly. Living in this way is considered normal in our society, but just because 'everyone' is doing it, it doesn't make it correct.

The inner drive to be happy is still there in the heart. It is the intuition that can sense there is more than what appears on the surface of our regular lives. We expend tremendous amounts of energy to get even a scrap of happiness. A fleeting moment of peace is often all we get. This even applies to the spiritual person who can often vacillate between moments of ecstasy followed by despair. Often I would experience these emotional swings during meditation (what I thought was meditation at the time).

This is the great effort of modern life – to be happy. The effort comes from the belief that happiness is found outside one's self. This distracts us from the purity and simplicity of heaven with the complication and struggle of seeking. This is the unfortunate state of the separate individual. The good news is that you are not this separate individual but the perfect unified expression of the Para/Self.

What are we struggling for?
We want to connect with the heaven that we lost in whatever way we can. We settle for a taste, because heaven is seen to be just a

dream or perhaps another possibility after death.

In Sanskrit, this dream and cloud of complexity is called samsara or apara (not Self). Samsara is the illusion or mirage of the world that appears. The word "appears" is the important point here. It is an appearance, regardless of how the separate individual relates to it. Appearances come and go in Para.

Separate individuals will find a conceptual heaven and spend time pondering it. This is considered a spiritual act, which is actually a very sad practice. It is sad from the perspective that this pondering usually lasts a lifetime or more. Rare is one who can see through its uselessness.

Heaven is the absence of a separate, individual you. As long as the appearance of a chooser lasts, the choice will be between heaven and hell. It is the chooser's job to make the 'right' choices to prepare for heaven or try to experience the best heaven has to offer. It does this to avoid hell.

The fact is, choosing for heaven or hell does not exist in Unity. Since there is no longer a chooser there is only choosing heaven since that is all there is. Choosing for hell is not Unity because hell is separation which cannot exist in reality.

There is only the Silence of God and being that. Heaven and hell may still continue to come and go within that Para/Unity, but there is no longer a separate choice to be made by 'somebody'. In other words you can walk into hell and feel the fire, but in reality see that it is only another experience happening within Unity. Don't get me wrong, hell is not fun (yes, I have been there), but what we are is bigger than that experience and the form it takes. Hopefully those who think they choose will choose heaven over hell because it just makes more sense. Until then we keep putting our hand in the fire.

Choosing is a spontaneous outpouring of love and surrender built into the reality of what we are. It is breathing. Do you choose to breathe or is breathing happening? Do you choose to pump your heart to stay alive? God is doing this for your body, thank God! When she stops beating your heart, do you have a choice?

That being said, this is only conceptual nonsense if you still believe you are a separate person, so forget about it and just choose for peace, stillness, love and Unity. Just ask yourself if what you are choosing is a concept that comes and goes, or is it permanent and unchanging. The stillness is the only choice. Finding out what that is is the only thing you need to know, and this is the path to UNITY!

The Silence and Unity are the same! When the Silence ceases to be an object of choice by saying to you, "Hello I am all that is," you are very, very close. Until then, we are getting ready. This preparation is part of the show, and most of us can relate to it to some degree.

Anyone who has ever fasted or done a cleanse can testify to the fact that the senses become more refined. Afterword, we taste the subtleties of a pear that we never noticed before. Even water can taste better. So fasting of the body is one way to purify the senses so that we may experience more clearly. (I personally don't do that anymore because I love food too much.)

Also, after fasting we might report having a clearer mind or being able to think with more focus. This is most noticeable when an alcoholic or drug addict stops using for a sufficient time to clear their senses. Suddenly there is a clarity that comes as the fog passes. This is referred to as "a moment of clarity".

There are those of us who fast as a spiritual quest to allow time for deep reflection or to go inward. We may go into Silence, or try not speaking to fast from the constant need to chatter and socialize. This reveals the deeper significance of the truth that gets avoided when we put our attention outward all the time.

There is a list of wild and interesting things people do to get their spiritual 'high'. Like the 'sweat lodge' or the 'Sun Dance'. It is amazing to me how many things we are willing to do to get close to the Divine. I met a native man from Calgary who said that he went through the 3 day Sun Dance. They stood him up next to a tree and put hooks through his chest so he couldn't sit down and rest. Then he danced around without food or water for three days until he was completely exhausted. After all that he said he had a spiritual high. That's not my style, although at the time I was intrigued.

One of the craziest things I personally have done was a sweat lodge in Mexico. At the time I considered myself a veteran meditator and spiritual warrior who could go through anything for 'the cause'. There was a group of us who had volunteered. At the time I was not really interested in this, but I was told that the chief of the Navajo Indians was coming and that he was the grandson of Geronimo. "Wow," I thought, "if ever there was a time to do a sweat lodge, this is it. This will be the Mack-daddy of all spiritual experiences!"

There were around nine of us who volunteered, 5 men and 4 women. We all knew each other because we belonged to the same meditation group. When he showed up I was shocked to see what looked like your average redneck guy, ball cap, dirty sports shirt, all roughed up, with a cigarette hanging out of his mouth.

"This guy is going to take me on a journey? Get outta here." So we all just chatted as he heated up the stones for the pit. He said that we could keep our underwear on but that we would be hiding our true self. He then gave an actual speech about being naked that lasted for an hour. I looked over at my friend who was even more macho, and as we locked eyes he said, "Not a freaking chance, dude!" I just laughed. The chief did have a good safety point, however; he said it could get so hot that it would melt the rubber band onto our stomachs, so we should at the very least fold the band on our underwear over.

Then before we came in he said that if it is too much for you just say so and we will let you out of the lodge. I thought, "He doesn't know who I am, I will go through this no problem. I don't want to be one of those wimpy people who can't take the heat."

Then we began. He was speaking in Spanish mostly, but I understood quite a lot since I had been in Mexico on long retreats many times. It was getting hotter and hotter and I felt like I was starting to die. I literally thought I was dying, but did not want to give up. I remember him saying, "It's really hot in here." "No shit," I thought, "maybe he overdid it since the expert himself was starting to complain." This can't be normal!

I was soaking wet and was starting to get delirious almost to the point of passing out. After ranting a while, he would say, "Abre la puerta," which means, "open the door." I got excited thinking, "He is going to let us out." Unfortunately it was just some sort of spiritual reference about the door to something or other.

And he just kept talking. I started getting weak and dizzy and leaning on my buddy's slimy arm. Then I started to panic, "I've got to get out of here, I am going to die, but I don't want to be the first to chicken out." Then he said, "Abre la puerta." Again I got excited but he just kept talking as it got hotter and hotter. Then something very interesting happened; one of the guys threw up all over the hot rocks. I thought, "Okay, now somebody will definitely get out." But guess what? Still nobody would move.

Around the fourth, "Abre la puerta," I couldn't stand it anymore. Screw being macho, I am going to die in here. "Stop! This is it! I want out of here!" I was so weak I thought for sure I would fall on the hot rocks as I stumbled over all the gross sweaty bodies.

I will tell you, when I passed the thick hot choking smoke into the cold air as I opened the door I was never so happy. I was in heaven. I fell down on the earth and rolled over soaking up Para (heaven). That was the last time I would do anything to detox, cleanse, or purify myself... screw that!

True, fasting is allowing what is to reveal itself. Since what is is Para, this can be revealed through bringing all the senses inward. This is the movement from apara (not self) to Para. This movement to Para frees up the inner sense (intuition). This inner sense comes through the fasting of the mind. By denying it the usual distractions of thinking we starve it, and therefore it has no choice but to start to detoxify.

At first (or for years) it might throw up, like the guy in the sweat lodge on the rocks. All sorts of stress-releasing thoughts and emotions may be released. It is our job to let them go as they come up. It could get stinky, but if we stay in the hut with our stuff there will just be more torment. Get some fresh air and get the heck out of there! Hold nothing.

The senses function quite naturally without the need of any manipulation. The self hears, sees, touches, smells and tastes the world. It does not need a 'middle man' or a separate person to make the senses function. You can go ahead and see this for yourself; when you follow each sense from the most external back into the origin, the functioning of life becomes an inner exploration.

This moving of the senses inward is what happens naturally when we come to rest in the Silence. Living in Heaven comes from the aliveness of the experience of this Silence and the functioning of the senses. An empty mind also functions in a simpler way to the other senses when there is no manipulation of thoughts and emotions as they come and go. The mind is left to revel and reveal in the pristine clarity of wisdom and the light of perfection. This is Para.

This is tasting heaven in the truest sense. How it looks may be different for each of us because we each are unique expressions. Our nervous systems once refined through Silence reveal our own slice of Para. This is our unique gift to the world. It has always been there and will sometimes sneak up on us during a moment of a 'peak experience' when we forget our limitations for a moment.

This is the spontaneous Unity of Para.

Being One with a Tree

Before we go and try to unite with everything, why not start with one thing at a time? How about a tree? Who doesn't want to be one with a tree?

Okay the first step is to go out and pick a tree. You can do this all in your head if you don't have a tree around you at this time. Don't cheat and do it on a plant, chair or a rock because the rules here are specific for trees only. I am just kidding; it works for most objects except for certain family members that push your buttons. Note: Rocks are much easier to become one with because they just sit there and don't move.

So, once you have a tree in your sights or inside your head, go ahead and get comfy. First let's look at what is apparently here and there. We have you, the tree, and the senses that perceive the tree. If you are doing this – if it is in your head – you have you, the image of your tree and then the image of your senses perceiving the tree. You might sense how the tree feels by touching it physically or by using your uni-intuition. You might have an idea of what the tree looks like in comparison with other trees you have seen. Is it more beautiful, smaller, denser? Is it more or less green than other trees, etc...?

Normally the separate individual will want to become one with the tree which is a lovely idea. Perhaps you can hug this tree (don't be shy, there are worse things that can and do happen everyday) and feel a connection with it. Go ahead and hug this tree and feel the love, if you wish. Yes, you are connected to your tree. Look at that, you are already a tree hugger and feeling your connection and we just started! By the way, this is a serious exercise about your freedom so whatever you do, do not laugh!

It is okay if you don't feel the love or connection, however, and just see a tree like any other tree. Either way being one with the tree will work because guess what? That is right, you are already one, we are simply removing the barrier to seeing the obvious.

The love and connection you feel with the tree is not Unity, however, nor is it oneness. It is the closest you can get to glimpsing oneness as long as you are still identified with being an individual wanting to be one with the tree. It is a great place to start. You can also do this with people too, or animals; basically you can intuit your oneness with all of creation.

I will warn you that if you go up to people and start hugging them to sense the connection it could end up badly for you. You might want to use discernment in this case and just feel it without acting on it. Also, just because animals run away from you doesn't necessarily mean that there is no love between you. Don't take it personally, they are just not used to that much love coming at them. It scares them.

In Unity there is only the Silence with an absence of concepts. What does this experience look like with you and the tree? The tree is still being perceived through the senses the same as any individual would see it. So what is the difference? The sages and the individual both see the tree in the same way, believe it or not.

In the Silence as it is now, there is no concept of a tree. You can check this out now. The Silence is eternally absent of concepts. Even the concepts of space such as 'here' and 'there' are nowhere in the Silence.

So with this new fresh way of seeing, what are you looking at? You can check this out now.

The senses still perceive, but something else is missing in the Silence. There is no longer identification with a tree. There is only Silence. The question is: What is this tree without identification? Listen without conceptualizing.

When there is Silence without concepts there is no separation. This is not because you have done anything profound or extraordinary, but because it is impossible to have a concept while experiencing the Silence in its purity. Incidentally this is why many of us can relate with seeing the beauty of nature and feeling the wonder and connection with everything. We attribute this to the beauty of the landscape and the 'things in nature', but that beauty is only a trigger to allow the mind to still and the intuition to reveal the Silence behind the things we see or the fresh air we breathe. Suddenly there is oneness. Even the identity of you as a concept disappears and what is left is the 'Peace of Being' in nature.

As you can see for yourself this is a very natural experience that can happen in any moment. Now we can see the motivation to go out into the wilderness and escape from the rat race, so to speak. As a child I remember being completely in joy, playing at my grandparents' cabin. Every rock and tree was totally alive within oneness. Life was not chopped up into little moments, but a seamless eternal adventure happening in nature.

The oneness of nature may seem more obvious when there is only that surrounding. The reality, however, is that the same peace of being is in the busy streets of your downtown or your local airport. The intuition is just as active and the oneness is just as alive. Go ahead and see.

Now you can do this same experiment on anything – including you. What are you without identification? Listen without conceptualizing.

In the purity of Silence there are no perceptions or mental images, only seeing what is. Perceptions and images come and go; and when we identify with them, we create our separate reality. Of course there is nothing wrong with this, but simultaneous to this is another possibility. A definition of a glimpse of Unity could be: When there is only Silence. This happens when the intuition of Unity reveals this Silence in full consciousness. This is seeing with innocence and freshness. Suddenly there is aliveness.

The amazing thing is until this point you have never really seen a tree or even your own self, but only another separate object to relate to. Strangely enough we do relate with our self as a separate object in the head. What are you in essence without thinking and imagining? Nobody can say except for you. This is the divine quest that leads to obviousness. Even being in love or connected to the tree is still an externality to the Unity you share with that tree. This is the ultimate intimacy waiting to be discovered and, like a secret treasure, will burst open when you see it.

Now comes the amazing part – to being one with the tree. Now that you are one with the tree you have an eternal relationship with it. Every time you see this tree it is a living expression of Unity that is eternally fresh.

This is all happening out of the very simple obviousness of Silence. Now to get a hint of what this could mean for 'you', let's look at stabilized Unity. Imagine if that same effortless experiencing of oneness applied to every one of the trillions of objects on the planet. Imagine having the same holy relationship with everything for eternity. You don't have to do all that by trying, but by effortlessly allowing what is.

This all came out of simple nothingness or the divine Silence.

So it is not really about you and the tree becoming one, but it's about seeing that both you and the tree are concepts floating in consciousness. This demonstrates how easy being free is because all there is is freedom or stories. Anything other than freedom only comes from identification with a concept. Of course you really and truly believe you are this concept. Interesting... you will have to prove that to me!

This is why even the most amazing teacher cannot give you Unity. She or he only helps you. It takes intense spiritual 'oomph' to jump into it fully. Who wants to permanently see that they were totally wrong their whole lives? Who wants to see that they actually have no idea about themselves at all? Not many people have enough oomph. Perhaps this is why Unity is so rare. The fact remains: it is your divine and sacred right to be free! In our tradition 'being truly human' is sometimes referred to as "full human consciousness". It is yours already!

The tree is more enlightened because the tree does not

conceptualize. Upon seeing this, everything becomes a mirror for you. Nature is showing us how to be one, like a tree. So go ahead and get some oomph; do it for the tree – not for me!

The Cosmic Duh!

The cosmic duh is the sudden and spontaneous waking up into Unity. It is Unity realizing itself as it is without a separate realizer. It is so obvious that it is really embarrassing that it wasn't seen before. This is why the angels shake their heads at you and go duh! Perhaps the old school angels say, "OM," because they are set in their ways.

Then you pretend to hang your head in shame, and think, "Wow, I had it all along."

Enlightenment does not feel like a well-deserved glass of water after a long run. It does not deserve the recognition of finally graduating university or landing that perfect job. In fact, enlightenment and embarrassment are quite similar in the holy instant of seeing for the 'first time'. This is only because of their obviousness.

The embarrassment is quickly replaced with awe and wonder. Thousands of lifetimes of being separate were a joke? This is unbelievable. "I cannot even blame the infinite anymore since all there is is infinity, I am THAT. Who can I blame? Myself? Why did I do it all?" Why mess about all these eons?

Why not?

Let us not forget that this is only a glimpse of Unity, albeit a conscious glimpse of Unity. Whether or not it becomes stable, we will wait and see. It could take years or perhaps you will never forget that you are free. Often amazing as it may sound, we forget this obviousness.

All you have to do is keep seeing! Is that difficult? If you do not conceptualize too much it should be a 'no brainer'. If you start thinking and doubting your 'experience' of Unity, it could be a 'brainer' for sure. No brain = no problem. KISS. (Keep it simple, silly.)

This one little glimpse will rewrite the entire history of humanity and the history of you as well. Your future and past are wiped out of existence. This is looking for glasses while they are on your face. This is screaming at your partner who lost your keys and then finding them in your pocket.

Seeing Unity is so clear that there is no doubt that all there is is God. It is not necessarily a profound, lights flashing and ascending into heaven kind of thing, although that could also happen simultaneously to it. It isn't even the fact that you are one with everything. It is more like, "So what," I am one with everything. DUH! It is not such a big deal because you see the cosmic obviousness of what is staring out of your face!

What is amazing is that you have apparently not been experiencing this freedom. This is what is amazing! How is that even possible? WOW! This is so embarrassing; I hope nobody noticed that my attention was off on Mars for the last 30 years. Where was I? Duh!

In this sense, samsara, illusion, drama and manifestation become an incredible source of entertainment and delight. You had me for so long, good one! Talk about a magnificent joke! God has been telling it for millennia and you finally got it. What is even funnier is that chances are you will forget it again! The angels' necks hurt from shaking their heads so much.

The Zen of Duh may last a second or two, but also does not ever have to leave at all. This is because Unity is all there is. For most there is a period of coming home into this permanently which can take years (lifetimes according to certain belief systems). It also depends on a few factors. There is really not much to do except enjoy it and bathe in the wonder of "No way!"

Good luck to you and for Para's sake DO NOT EVER take a single thing seriously (except for this statement), that is unless you like pain.

Wake Up and Smell the Coffee, or Tea, if Coffee is not Your Cup of Tea

I look forward to my morning cup of coffee. Of all the thoughts that have gone through my head during the day, this one is usually the first. It gets me up out of bed. The smell of coffee gets me going, heck even the thought of the smell of coffee gets me revved up. I admit it I am an addict, but the first step is to admit it. The truth is I have been in denial my whole life when it comes to addiction. I didn't want to believe it, but after many times trying to quit my various addictions I have come to accept it.

My father told me, "Son, if you are like me you are an addict; you have addiction in your genetics on both sides of your family. You have an addictive personality." Of course I didn't believe him because, "I have things in control." So I would think, "I am more powerful than that!" I have been addicted to God, movies, Buddha, Jesus, gurus, thoughts, tacos, sugar, energies, sex, drugs, crystals, TV, chips, pop, cigarettes, and now have refined my addiction to Silence and coffee.

My favorite addiction of all time was to myself. I was addicted to my thoughts and my feelings because they surrounded the story of me. Thinking became my ultimate addiction and as a result my inner and outer life became reflective of it. Later when I saw the futility and helplessness of being happy through normal addictions, I turned to God and spirituality for the solution. Then the addiction turned into a fanaticism for truth and God. I turned God and truth into concept and then built my identity around it. I became addicted to being enlightened or a "wannabe yogi" as my Teacher said.

The split between the normal me and this spiritual me became too great for me to handle. I wanted to repress or kill anything that was not living up to my idea of truth. The more I conceptualized the truth or refined it, the more I felt disconnected from it as a living reality. The feeling of being hallow increased as I simply could not fill that vacuum inside. It was like a hungry monster was begging to get fed but nothing could satisfy it. Once I learned how to focus on the Silence through the practice of meditation it became obvious as to how addicted I was to thinking. I was self-absorbed with my story. This thinking addiction always led to pain, and I did not know how to stop it.

When I stopped thinking (miraculously) even for an instant the pain disappeared, and there was peace. You would think that this would become clear immediately, but it took thousands of times of putting my hand in the fire before I saw the connection.

When the clarity arose that the Silence leads to the peace of contentment and the end of addiction, I became addicted to the Silence. As far as addictions go this one is very sweet and harmless. Only the best of addictions frees you from further addiction. I then saw my addictive nature as a blessing, in a way almost like a passion. The addiction turned into a passion for the joy of self-discovery. The unhealthy obsession of the spiritual ego dissolved into the passion for aliveness or tasting of truth. Eventually the energy of being addicted to thinking shifted as the 'me' center was no longer being supported by it. The cycle of me/thinking/addiction was dissolved into exploring the awe of Being as it is.

Once this 'me' gets dissolved, then there is only the impersonal thinking addiction which is something that can happen when one goes on unconscious or on 'auto-puppet' mode. This slipping is easy to see and therefore deal with as we become familiar with the cycle. As my Teacher says, "By focusing on the conscious thinking, the unconscious thinking takes care of itself." This means by being aware of those moments when we are off, we can come back to the Silence.

In other words, by recognizing when you are thinking, you can stop – assuming you have a tool to go inward – and be still or cease thinking. This creates a new habit of focusing attention on the Silence, which, over time, helps dissolve the addiction or the addiction to the addiction. You never force yourself to stop thinking on a path of Joy because by putting attention on the Silence the mind, with practice, automatically prefers listening and being quiet. The Silence is everything the mind wants. Again, this is difficult to do without a valid meditation technique. As you know the stress of life adds up, and thinking is just happening. So usually we need a tool to dissolve this stress and give us the option to choose peace. When we do this, those times when we unconsciously drift off into never-land also eventually cease. In Unity the habit of thinking is no longer a big deal. When it happens it does not distract the attention away from the Silence.

Dealing with addictions is hard enough when the separate individual is involved. Surrendering to the divine is a wonderful way to see the lack of control this inner addict has.

Waking up does not necessarily dissolve the personality's addictions. This is especially true if the character is predisposed to them. Waking up dissolves the separate addict that has a story of addictions, not necessarily the addiction itself. Seeing through the story of 'me' and 'my' addiction frees us from separation, but not the characteristics that are a part of programming the 'me'.

That being said, we can wake up one day without the usual desire for what we were addicted to. Depending on the person, this can happen through going to the traditional 12-step program or 'cold turkey'. It can also be the spontaneous result of the cosmic Oomph or Holy Spirit. These are my favorite ways to quit, but don't hold your breath waiting for them to save you. In Unity there is no judgment around addictions because they are no longer seen as personal. By seeing with innocence we can learn to accept the energy around it regardless of whether or not it goes away. By channeling this energy into the Silence, we make good use of it. Maybe it transforms into passion?

Note: It is very interesting to notice that the 12-step program applied to recovering addicts has the two main foundations for Unity in the steps. The steps of meditation and surrender to a higher power are the keys to freedom. It is no wonder these programs have such tremendous power and success. Also note that by being with people who have the same focus such as 'to heal', 'to support', 'to share' the popcorn effect is amplified. This is like being in the company of sages who are supportive of Unity and the givers of the highest good imaginable.

Glimpses of Unity versus Stabilized Unity

Glimpses of Unity are wonderful, but they come and go just like everything does. They are the seeing into or 'In sights' into the Unity of All there is. Of course for the spiritual person, they seem to be special and wonderful, which then attract us to chase after these moments like objects. This can be a double-edged sword. God has 'got you' at that point. The end is inevitable; whether in a moment or a thousand years, you will recognize your divine inheritance.

After the cosmic duh, or seeing that there is only THIS, Unity can become stable or permanent.

For some this is an easy and obvious transition, but for others it can be a journey of surrender and allowing until the obvious becomes constant. Perhaps it is because of the habit of conditioning that we have endured in our lives or for thousands of lives that turns this into another process. We need not concern ourselves with it, however, since it is no longer about our effort or strength of will. More importantly it is not about 'us' at all. Any effort after that point can be putting our self in our own way. It is useful to remember the way of nothing that has nothing in the way since it is all in the hands of God now.

Even though the 'glimpse' is now a memory, this does not negate the impact it can have on the path. It is an insight into Unity as it is now. Keep in mind that the process of unification is only conceptual or 'a story'. In some ways it can be seen as the final story. Hearing that it is a story does not necessarily help to stabilize it, but it is worth a shot.

In another sense, it still is not a process because 'you' have nothing to do with it. Maybe that makes it seem longer to stabilize. The separate individual might be trying to control or manipulate the experience (it turns the glimpse into an experience or object to be attained) based on a memory of the experience as it happened 'to you' in the past. Of course this is illusory and if you believe it then you might have to go a ways down the path to realize this.

Unity cannot be experienced. This is where words can be deceiving. I chose the word glimpse because it implies seeing into Unity. This is not experienced by you but seen or glimpsed when you, as a separate subject, are not there. It is the subjectivity of all there is. It is all that is happening now.

The Unity 'experience' is dissolution of you. It is not an actual 'experience' because experiences happen to 'someone'. Without you there, there is only an experiencing of ONENESS.

Stabilization happens through constantly seeing into what is obviously THIS oneness without separation. The Silence has always been the answer and this is still the only answer. All is stillness without you there. Since there is a basic habit of conceptualization in the average person this can and will come up 'after' the glimpse of Unity has happened (except in the famous rare cases, if they truly exist). Doubts can come up and thinking becomes tempting. When you do these things out of habit they tend to shrink the awareness of Unity. This is the separate subject re-creating itself. Forget about doing anything about this because it is part of the process, from a linear point of view.

Unity is ongoing infinite aliveness that is pure inspiration and clarity. In other words, the more consciousness is aware of Unity, the easier it is to rest there. Without a separate individual it is easy because that is in essence naturalness and simplicity.

The key is to forget about what that looks like since it cannot be known. It is new territory and must be experienced with innocence. All maps get thrown out the window along with the GPS of inner dialogue. "Turn right here into allowing, stop and ignore the mind here," the mind says. Of course, whether or not this happens who knows? Again it's worth a shot to suggest innocence.

During the process of stabilization reality begins to hit the stage. What this means is what you had thought 'being enlightened' would look like is now over and you are seeing firsthand the hard facts of Unity.

Maybe you thought you would never feel anything other than Peace?

Maybe you thought you would be invincible or get super powers and read the minds of others?

Maybe you thought you would never have any more thoughts period?

Maybe you thought it would be easy?

Maybe you thought all your problems would just fly away?

The list of Unity concepts is endless, and when it happens apparently to 'you', you will be faced with everything that you still believe about what Unity is in reality.

I could also point out that anything that you can come up with has 'the separate you' as the center. The point of Unity is: NO YOU. Therefore, who are 'you' to decide what it looks like? You have nothing to do with it. This is not in the "I am going to get enlightened manual." It is not as great as you thought it was; but then again, it is probably far better in ways you could not have imagined.

Stabilizing Unity is allowing what is. In the light of seeing what is, there is only THIS. Unity teaches you what you are versus what you appear to be in the story. Stabilizing Unity is about allowing all of you to appear; whether or not you consider it the ego is irrelevant to UNITY. Unity has no positions about ego or whether or not 'you' appear. Bear in mind that 'ego' and 'you' are merely concepts at this point.

This can be scary. This is also not mentioned in the manual because no one would bother to seek it if they knew they had no control over the outcome. Instead we think this 'me' will become enlightened in all its glorious buttery, sugary goodness and get a yummy crown of sweetness. In other words, the separate person can come into the picture to try to help you stabilize your 'experience' of Unity. It is there to make sure you get it right when in truth you can only get it wrong! Seeing into the humorousness of this dance of 'you' and 'no you' will go a long way into the stabilization process.

This reminds me of a fellow student who was talking about the thoughts in his head. He kept noticing the thoughts, "We are getting close to freedom," "We are almost there." Then he started to wonder, "Who are the 'WE'?" When he saw this he just laughed at the hysterical 'WE' that were in his head trying to guide him to freedom. Not taking anything seriously is a reliable key.

This is after all a joke. If all there is is Unity, then Unity of what with what? Unity implies the unification of something with something else, does it not? This is ridiculous. This is so simple I can't tell you. Literally I can't tell you!

The bottom line is there is only THIS and anything you do will only get in the way. My favorite concept is nothing, or no thing. There is nothing else to say.

I am Not Enlightened, But Neither are You, So There

When I say this to certain people who have heard my story secondhand they get a look of disappointment on their face. This is understandable. One of my favorite things to do was to be in the presence of an enlightened one. This, however, was also one of my biggest mistakes. Until separation is gone, we can't help but put at least a little bit of enlightenment on someone or something else.

Enlightenment does not happen to a personality, body or individual. Enlightenment happens despite all these concepts. You are not in Unity, all there is is Unity.

Unity is the changeless reality behind this insane world. That is an important distinction to make, as it is a misconception to think otherwise. There is nothing for you there to grab, which is a tragedy for he who would grab. At least you can hold other goals, like money or a sexy partner. Enlightenment cannot be held. It is a 50,000 ton weight, and a speck of dust at the same time. Trying to hold it is just funny. It is even funnier to watch other people try to hold it.

You would think that infinite treasure would be given to you, as you are exalted into a throne with your very own crown of enlightened glory. That is complete shit! Of course I would never have been seeking if I did not believe that as well. We can't help it, it is just part of the story.

Enlightenment has nothing to do with you or me because that is all there is. Unity is all there is and within the story or dream certain separate individuals disappear into nothingness. Does this sound like fun for the individual? Not really. Is death fun for you? Only the God of death will have fun and dance on your pretend head. So don't be deceived because, for one thing, you will chase after this thing that does not exist for a thousand lifetimes. My wish for you is that this doesn't happen. This is why I recommended a path of joy similar to the Bright Path. Direct and simple is the way to go!

You exist as consciousness, but what is that? When seeing through to the heart of reality, it is seen that all there is is Unity without any special acknowledgement. What would seek after acknowledgment? That's right. If everyone recognized there was only Unity, the big goal in life would be to try to figure out how to be separate just for the fun of it.

Hey, wait a minute; maybe that is what happened to all of us in the first place?

Stop pretending or keep enjoying your story, but at least get off the fence and decide what you want. Concepts or freedom, it's that simple.

God

To the separate individual God is a concept. In Unity, God is all there is. God is a very important concept because it gives the seeker something to look for. I began my quest just like this. I thought I would die if I did not find God in this lifetime. If I had not had that energy pushing me towards that quest who knows what would have happened.

It is very interesting that each individual comes about the search in infinitely different ways; not everyone is a fanatic like me. My partner Shanti, for example, had never given any serious thought to God or spiritual matters, but was simply pointed to meditation as something that could help her become happier. It was not a life or death thing for her. It was just listening to good advice. Yet regardless of appearances, the goal is the same. It begins and ends in the oneness of Unity. This is the magic of God in that whatever road you take ends up taking you home. Some take the 'long' road, but what is a long time compared to eternity?

I felt urgency like I literally had no choice but to search in the traditional spiritual sense. I searched for God on the outside as an object. It seemed like I had been looking forever (perhaps even in past lives). This longing was painful, but also was felt as a spiritual intensity or push at the same time.

I went to India to find God. I heard He was in a specific body there, so I went to see that body. When I could not see God there I went to another body. Then I forgot about bodies and started looking for God in sacred places. When that didn't work I looked inside at my concepts of God. Yet underlying the search was the uni-intuitive nature that I was fooling myself by looking outside.

I was addicted to searching for God. I thought I was looking for something for me, but what I truly wanted was the absence of me. Ironically I was seeking my own death, yet at the same time was avoiding this death at all costs by seeking. Make no mistake – that is the purpose of seeking! We seek to avoid God and to perpetuate the story of 'me'. This is the path of the Gods.

When enough is enough and it is no longer satisfying to see God in this and that, there is a kind of courage, honesty or readiness that swells up. The cosmic oomph sweeps in. This is the seeking for and/or experiencing of God as what is non-conceptual. This is God as all there is without concepts.

I had an internal battle with my concept of God that lasted many years. It was my addiction to finding the ultimate treasure that would make me special and finally worthy of the Love of God. Little did I know that the still quiet voice was right all along. I was only delaying what was always and eternally available. This is LOVE and the true meaning that God is LOVE. What greater gift could God give you other than God as it is? Anything else would just be another ugly sweater we have to be thankful for. No thanks!

Knitting It All Together Like Grandma Used To Do

Both my grandma and great-grandma were great knitters. My great-grandma would knit us all these little booties for our feet cause during winter it could get pretty cold in Calgary. Whenever I would see them rocking back and forth in their chairs I couldn't believe how quick and efficient they were pushing those needles around, weaving in and out of the yarn. I said, "Grandma, how do you do that, it looks so hard!" She said, "It's easy once you know how, it becomes like second nature." I never learned how to knit, but I always enjoyed watching them.

Like knitting the bootie becomes second nature for the grandma, all the pieces to the puzzle fall into place in Unity. At first 'youknittea' seems like a bunch of yarn all tangled up in our heads and hearts. We hope at some point it will make sense and hope it will become second nature. For now we fake it until we make it. All the conceptual puzzle pieces of youknittea become Unity when there is a direct seeing into the simplicity of what you are. This happens effortlessly, like grandma knitting. She does not think about how to knit, the knitter is gone from the equation. She is rocking with the chair, yarn, needles, and all there is is the knitting-ness happening. She may have a few thoughts floating by, but the possibility is for the total effort-lessness of knitting to happen. When this does, the knitter and the grandma disappear into Unity. This makes grandma happy!

The process of unification is like this: at first we are in the process of unifying ourselves because we heard that it is possible to have what we truly want more than anything – such as peace or freedom. Then we seek understanding through meditation, books, teachers and maybe a teaching. Then we start knitting it all together. Sometimes instead of a full boot we make part of a toe, but with practice we get better and better. Finally the process of knitting or unification becomes second nature and all that is left is the final surrender into the unknown Teacher of Silence as it says, "Leap." The unifier, the process of Unification and Unity become absolute and all is second nature.

Thanks, Grandma, for teaching me the truth in your own way and making the best breakfast I have ever had!

Can You Lose Your Unity?

The answer to this question is yes and no. Whoops! There it goes. It seems hysterical to think that you can lose all there is, yet isn't the case for the majority of humanity in the first place? We have all lost it; yes we have done the impossible. God has said, "Okay I am going to give you everything, but whatever you do, don't lose it or it might take a while to find it." Like a million years in most cases.

If it is true that all there is is Unity, then we must have lost it somewhere. We have already lost all there is by forgetting our true nature. So in a very real sense what does anyone have to lose by going after his or her highest desire (i.e. peace, fulfillment, connection, etc)? The discussion here is not about how we lost it originally, however, but what happens after you find it again.

The question is: after becoming free and stabilizing Unity can you lose it? The answer is yes, you can forget. This is more common than one might imagine – especially for those people who either were born enlightened or 'popped' without any teaching or meditation practice. Since there is no path and in some cases no Teacher (a Teacher meaning a Sage that guides one to Unity – helps one see the obvious, that they are already free), there is no way to stay on track or to know if you fall off. The mind is so subtle and tricky that self-referral becomes almost impossible. How can an insane mind determine the level of insanity or sanity in itself? Make no mistake; if the separate self has been re-engaged and has taken a position of control or authority, it is already too late. You forgot. This does not mean you cannot remember this instant, however, but as long as you are lost it becomes harder and harder to find the way back. This is the black and white of Unity and separation, knowledge and ignorance, Silence and conceptualizing. To be with one is to be without the other.

The only reference after Unity for what is happening is the mind of the 'one' in Unity. This is the value of being in the company of sages or wise ones. This is the greatest assurance and insurance although there are no absolute guarantees. This quest is dangerous, which is why it is so fun and such a satisfying adventure. Since the 'one' in Unity no longer cares about what is happening, a fall into separation can also appear to be okay. In fact the 'one' in Unity is correct because this falling out is totally okay since there is no real separation. Separation at this point is seen – though if you follow the old habits of thinking-ness by re-identifying with doubts, stories and me-centeredness, the separation into subject and object can reappear and the 'one' forgets the experiencing of Unity. Attention and focus are now back onto an imagined subject. This can be temporary or permanent in terms of a lifetime.

What can we do to prevent this besides surrounding ourselves with sages?

It is rare to 'pop' if we have not done the work. Fortunately, in our case the work is actually what saves us from the possibility of forgetting in the first place. This inner work also gives us the tools to help or resonate with others along their spiritual paths. Of course on a path of joy the work is the highest enjoyment and a constant reminder of what is important. The fact is that as long as there is a belief in a separate individual who will have 'it' then lose 'it', the losing of this Unity will appear to happen. This is the glimpse of Unity that comes and goes. When the 'you' center disappears you have it, when the 'you' returns you lose it. It is only this silly perception of the mind that sees the getting and losing of Unity as a slippery object.

After stabilization, or perhaps you could say relative stabilization, since as yet it is not mountain-like stable, a belief, doubt, or concept can start to take attention away from the Silence. This can be a precursor to identification with the ego. Usually the sage is so familiar with 'the work' of exploring the Silence that there is no interest in such conceptualization. For one, it becomes more painful to engage that type of egoic thinking. This extreme pain becomes a sign that the attention has shifted from reality to unreality. All that is required is to gently and without taking it seriously put attention on the Silence.

The Silence at this point is not an object, but all there is. Therefore it becomes easy to see that there has been a simple misidentification. This is not a problem and in fact can happen for a long time after 'popping' into Unity. This is a part of becoming like a rock of stillness. The idea that freedom or enlightenment is something like an event that once it happens is over is a wonderful idea, but there is more to this than meets the eye. I myself have fallen into this concept. I had a feeling that I deserved a break after these thousands of lifetimes struggling to get it and got lazy.

Often it can be this sense of giving up the sharpness of attentiveness to reality – as if it takes effort. It does not take effort to have attention on the totality of the Silence, but it does take attention; attention with a Love of the Silence is an effortless alertness. A misunderstanding of this can mean becoming lazy and allowing the attention to wander off. This can be natural, but if we choose to stop caring about what is important, we can re-create the old habits of little self-absorption.

It would seem crazy once there is an ongoing stabilized Unity to choose anything else. Still, the possibility exists for the separate individual to arise through the arrogance of being 'someone' again. This especially happens if the individual thinks that Unity is something special that happened to them. The ownership of Unity as 'mine' of course is not consciously experiencing Unity because it is impossible to own anything separate. In some cases the holding onto the idea of 'being free' can be a precursor to a sort of falling out of Unity. This is not a bad or evil experience, but is just a misunderstanding or misidentification.

An 'oops', if you will.

In some cases, it is quickly seen as just another thought, but in others – especially without guidance or being surrounded by conscious people – it becomes a trap. This trap is the trap of 'being an enlightened person'. Then these people write books, grab a microphone and head out onto the guru circuit screaming quietly, "Look at me! I know what I am talking about!" underneath their enlightened appearance.

Unity has never actually occurred, since the ownership of experience was still there. Unity does not happen to an individual; Unity is the disappearance of the individual. The humility of Unity is the stabilization of it because it is seen that Unity was never yours as an object and therefore cannot be lost. Unity belongs to everything and includes everyone. Unity is obvious in this sense. When Unity is solid it becomes difficult to lose as long as conceptualizing is kept in check.

That being said, vigilance of choice does seem to become more important than one would think. Making a decision to consciously think is not a good idea. The good news is that the universe uses a tool to get you back on the Unity track... the universal term for this is pain. Choosing to think becomes a thousand times more painful and exhausting in Unity. In ignorance it seems effortless to think; now it is the reverse. It is effortless to BE, but not to think.

Deciding to identify with that which comes and goes instead of the changeless can mean forgetting reality. This is where being in holy company is very important in order to maintain clarity and direction. In some ways 'popping into Unity' is like being reborn – without clear guidance, it can be easy to slip into old patterns as they come up.

Being in Unity does not mean transcending being human and all that goes along with it. It may be seen like this for a while, though. In fact, it is the full-on allowing of all that was previously avoided in being human. The Silence of Unity is the innocent accepting of every possibility within the human condition, it says "Yes" to everything. Old patterns, programs and conditionings come up to be seen for what they are. They are seen in the light of love and acceptance.

Now emotions are not avoided or repressed but embraced with love. The depth of sorrow can be felt to the core like squeezing the water from a sponge... it is all aliveness in expression. The controller of emotions has left the building. If there is a sense of being beyond or having something that someone else doesn't, that is the separate individual creeping back into play. There is nothing to fear in the loss of Unity because it cannot actually be lost but simply misunderstood. Sometimes it is necessary to stray from reality for a while to see it for what it is. This is usually when I start hitting my head on things 'by accident'. At this point I would suggest praying to the universe to slap you when you get off track. Trust me, you want to be slapped or at least nudged in the 'right' direction – Silence – the other alternative is not so sweet. This can include things such as dreaming you're a sheep, errr, I mean asleep.

A clear Teacher can help to guide the student through the subtleties of this and support them. Now more than ever, guidance is important. A sense of being beyond is tempting for the ego and it wants the power that that would bring. True power, however, is humble surrender not ownership.

Unity is infinite and will continue to reveal the divine relationship forever. Again, the first step on a path of joy is learning not to take things seriously. This attitude applies to Unity as well. Seeing in this new perspective is joyful and as long as not taking things seriously is kept in one's awareness, it is a seamless dance of ever-revealing wonder. Allowing ourselves to fall down and make mistakes is part of it while we have a puppet-body with all its strange and wonderful characteristics. The freedom comes when we understand there is nothing we have to do or be in order to 'be' in Unity. It is only what is without separation. Letting go of what that looks like to you is part of the dance and is absolutely liberating with each step taken, as well as all of the steps missed, tripped over or fallen down and hitting your nose on the floor.

In this day and age we are not living in caves having to do it alone. We are helping each other because there is no 'each other' – there is only oneness – only Unity. Praise the lord, Krishna, baby Jesus or whatever your God is!

Popping into Unity

'Pop' and that's it. When the conditions are right, we pop. It can happen right now in the Silence. What is there awareness of now? Is there awareness of the Silence or a story?

It is this easy to see through the tiny veil of separation. By exploring the Silence we see that that is all that is required. Being on a Path of Joy and seeing the illusion of all concepts are the fruits of the pop. It all begins and ends in Silence. Seeing into this Silence is everything.

The problem for the seeker is the concept of what that popping actually is. Even if the seeker has been educated and 'heard the truth', the subtle idea of what popping into enlightenment looks like keeps us from getting the cookie from the cookie jar. Any sane person who has glimpsed the freedom from exploring the Silence would want the cookie – that's for sure. There is nothing wrong with that desire as long as the cookies are homemade and not artificial. Without the desire for the cookie, popping would be a random stroke of good luck like winning the lottery. There is a better chance of getting struck by lightning. If you're interested in getting hit by lightning, your chances are even better if you wait for a stormy night, then wrap yourself in tin foil, grab a long metal pole and run around chasing the flash of lightning.

In a similar way – like being naked, not wrapping yourself in tin foil – we can do things to get ready for the pop. Some things are more useful than others. I actually believed that popping into enlightenment was similar to being hit with lightning at one point during my searching career. A beam of light would get brighter and brighter and then "Ka Pow!" – A bolt from god would smash though my chakras shaking them to the core and my eyes would roll back in my head as I levitated on a cloud of bliss while the omniscience of the universe poured into me... I

Without You There: The Zen of Unity

AM GOD. Take that you little humans… hahaha.

Usually in meditation, the light would get brighter and brighter and my heart would race, "Here it comes," then I would open my eyes to see that the sun was just shining in my face through the window… "Damn it, almost had it!" Or I would hear the OM and start to tear up with joy only to realize it was the humming of the refrigerator.

Whenever I did have those light experiences, of white light etc I would chase them with intensity. Of course this would also push them away. What do these wonderful experiences mean?

Is Kundalini a sign I am getting close?

Perhaps I am getting further away because these apparently amazing experiences happen less and less these days. What experience has shown – and not just my experience, but the experiences of many explorers – is that these fantastic experiences are not at all necessary for popping or signs that popping will happen. They can and do occur as a part of a popping at times depending on the particular nervous system and the environment. These phenomena are only side effects or appearances happening. They are neither good nor bad. They are simply cool.

I taught a course once with a teacher named Narain. He is one of my all time favorite guys because he is wise, gentle and humble. At the time, he had been around and had a lot more experience teaching than I had. I was a little intimidated to be side-by-side with him, but he just made everyone including me feel totally at ease in his presence. After we went though some instructions and gave the first technique of the Bright Path, we closed our eyes to ascend. Ascend in this tradition is another word for meditate on or rise beyond the mind. When we opened our eyes, I looked over and he had tears coming down his face. I remember thinking, "Jesus, what happened to him." All I experienced was nothing and thoughts.

After we finished teaching I asked him, "Dude, what happened to you in there?" He said, "I closed my eyes and all of a sudden I could see my crown chakra, there were thousands of petals. Then I started to move into one of them and whole universes were inside one of the petals. Then when we opened our eyes I could see everyone's chakra system filled with light and these orbs were spinning around each of us."

I thought, "Holy shit! Who is this guy?" He must be from another planet. If I would have chased after that experience I would still be flying around somewhere, but certainly nowhere close to being what I am. The lesson for me became clear because of the extreme contrast at that moment and the truly humble nature of Narain. It was obvious to me that what happened came and went for him and that it was not special, but just a cool experience he had. I saw that all that mattered was what I am experiencing because that is all there is for me.

These experiences are not to be avoided or feared just because they are perceived as abnormally fantastic. There is nothing wrong with fireworks and angels and such. If seen for what they are, there is never a problem with getting distracted or caught up with the display. Making it special or waiting for them as an excuse to pop is just a waste of time, however.

The Silence does not care what is happening; only the ego has a serious opinion about such things. We all have the preference of experience, but to resist what is happening is an invitation to delay our peace. This is the beauty of allowing all experiences, including the glimpse of Unity to come and go.

The confusion for the seeker is in seeing what is to be understood by 'popping'. Of course popping into Unity is a concept for the seeker that can easily be misinterpreted. The word pop sounds like an event that will happen to 'me'. This puts a limit on popping. Confusion is caused by thinking. Without thinking or conceptualizing, popping into Unity can begin to take on a fresh new aliveness. Instead of a single one-time pop, the pop can be an ongoing and current popping-ness that has no end.

Popping can be seen as an event like the 'God-struck (luck)' of enlightenment. It can be seen as a single strike or multiple strikes happening in a lifetime. Perhaps you have had some of them. If we relate popping with the extraordinary, however, we miss the huge reality that is already popping into Unity. We can see the aliveness popping right now.

Popping is much more common than we think. The further 'you' go, the more you see that popping is happening not just as tiny events revealing pieces of freedom, but that all there is is a continuing aliveness of popping continually.

Take for example your average everyday normal Joe. During that day Joe pops in and out of awareness, sometimes thinking about his favorite sports team losing their last outing, and then there are moments of Silence.

These moments of Silence are very normal, but since the seeker is looking for the fantastic strike of lightning, they can miss the treasure already present. The meditator and/or ascender (one who rises beyond) has an opportunity that Joe is not aware of. This chance enables her or him to see the living 'popping-ness' of Unity. Instead of unconscious moments of popping into the Silence of not thinking, awareness catches the sublime-ness of the underlying Unity; and before it's known, we are already popping into this state of not thinking consciously.

For almost everyone, this seems like a random pop into Silence because there is not an active desire to do so. The joke is that once the desire gets ignited for the seeker to be free – this could also be considered a 'pop' – this Silence is usually completely neglected at first. It is not seen as valuable.

I spent years avoiding the pop simply because I had no clear direction of focus. My attention was all over the place and then suddenly and randomly I would pop into peace. The popping into peace and Unity was happening all the time, but it had no importance to me since I didn't know that it was important. What

I wanted was the fantastic popping of enlightenment. Instead of seeing the obvious, I put my energy into conceptualizing what I thought enlightenment was and then waited for that concept to come and awaken me. To me, if I could figure it out or refine my intellect enough, it would happen. Of course not everyone does this.

Popping is not something that needs to happen to get to Unity. Popping into Unity is seeing that all there is is the popping. The only question is whether or not we are aware of it. Being aware of the Silence we see the dance of popping in and out until we are only popping in and in and in. This is aliveness. This is the popcorn effect.

The opportunity for the seeker is to see that what they are is already jumping in. The gift is given a thousand times a day, but goes unnoticed. We neglect it as too familiar because it is not registered by a mind that is craving the fantastic. The irony of course is that the Silence is fantastic, but absolutely out of the realm of what we think it should look like. The mind has no clue. It is too familiar simply because it is what we are. To see it is to POP. To BE it is popping into Unity.

A Unity Story

Unity is beyond perception. When describing it in words (especially as a story), it is like taking a snapshot from the perception of the instant it is taken. This is an attempt to take that snapshot. What I have noticed is that the perception of Unity changes as clarity seems to unfold. The story I would have told ten years ago is not the same as two years ago and will be different a year from now since clarity is current and continuous. I feel it is important to emphasize that Unity is simple but indescribable. It is very big because it is about your true nature. Perhaps if we take all of our pictures and put them together we would have a fuller picture of how it unfolds. I have seen it unfold in different ways so who can say one story is better than another. They are just stories.

I have heard it explained as a single event that once done was complete. For example you're walking down the street to get a Slurpee. While you are walking, you notice that you are not moving your body; it is as if it is on automatic pilot. Then you look down at your feet and see that they are not your feet, then bam! You hit your head on the pole leading up to the stop sign (don't attempt this!) and there is only Bliss. Suddenly 'you' are enlightened.

I have also heard it explained as a very gradual progression. From this perspective it seems to be both sudden and gradual. Usually this is a compilation of Unity glimpses (sounds like a soundtrack from the Unity DVD) that were not even necessarily realized as such until later. This is the change in perception I am referring to as the Unity story unfolds. At some point in this story there is the realization that there is no separation and then Bam! 'You' are enlightened. This sudden Unity pop happens almost always after some time exploring the Silence.

I think it is most common in the world for the popping to

occur on a path of joy. This is where the Silence has become very familiar through the path and the guidance received. This path is very clear and direct. The advantage of this instead of just popping on your way to the convenience store (besides the fact that it is more rare than winning the lottery five times in one day) is that it is more likely to be stabilized. Also it is easier to guide others in that direction once it happens, which is the whole point of waking up. Service is the point.

Often I have seen the poppers without a path say wonderful things and inspire, but not really have anything practical to do since they have no idea what they did themselves. This does not invalidate the 'experience', but points to the difficulty in sharing or pointing to it for the benefit of others. Being in the presence of the sage can be of benefit; there is no doubt about that. Many people sat around Ramana Maharishi without a single word being said. This went on for years until the teaching started; at least teaching in terms of communicating or pointing out truth in words as well as sitting in Silence.

So how is the question the seeker needs to discover. Saying things like "just be still" or "watch your thoughts" can appear useful; but without a direct path of moving from separation into freedom in a step-by-step manner, it is difficult to see what actually works. This is the problem for the seeker who searches for advice from the 'no path' poppers. Since there has not been a path to pop, it becomes a matter of 'nothing you can do but wait'.

If you are okay with waiting then of course that is fine, but having a practical and reliable way to explore the Silence, in my opinion, is the simplest and easiest way to go. A path of joy is an active and alive dance, which is continually engaging truth. This path is not abstract, but very practical and you could even say mechanical in that it is consistent and repeatable.

My story has been changing over the years. That is not because I was lying, I promise you I was being honest throughout, but that the view has gotten larger and more encompassing, a little more eternal, if you will.

Somehow the past has changed even though the events have not. The story has become clearer, at least in perception. It seems strange to say, but my past is actually getting better. This makes me laugh since I have spent the majority of my life trying to get over it. The story is getting better. Again, this seems very weird as I write it, but there is no other way I can think of to describe it. It is as if consciousness is moving through time and space into the story to bring more light into it. It is not changing the events in the story, but lightening them up in some way to bring the clarity of Unity into them.

The Unity story is a story about waking up. In a way we all have a Unity story because it can be seen as the story of 'one day I will be in Unity', or 'I will never be in Unity', or even 'what the heck is Unity anyway?' All of these stories are happening in Unity. Being in the process of Unity as well as waking up into Unity is also a story happening in Unity. In other words there is the aliveness of it and the perception of it.

To the separate individual seeking enlightenment, it is apparent that the story of 'how I woke up' would be preferable to 'how I didn't make it'. If you are on 'a path' you have a Unity story. The question is: where are you on it? Are you farther from or closer to Unity and freedom?

In Unity, the story is no longer important or even noticed anymore. You could say it has dissolved because it is of no more interest. It is much more enjoyable to play in the Silence than to reflect on the changing story.

Throughout this journey I have been a kind of connoisseur when it comes to observing Unity stories. Each one has a unique flavor. This makes sense since we are so different in character. When listening to them throughout my life I would try to pin down the formula so I could do the same thing as they did. Often this was very difficult, as I would hear contradictions in the different stories and also within the same story of one sage. These contradictions or paradoxes are a necessary part of describing the indescribable 'experience' of Unity. It is described in dualistic terms, which is why the resonance with what is is so important. The first and last teaching of Unity is... Silence.

This is why when listening to stories, especially of Unity, it is most wise to listen without trying to take in a formula. There is a natural resonance or intuitiveness that shines through the story because it is your story as well. All the Unity stories have common threads or similarities that can be seen through our own experience and through the universal 'things' that happen before and after Unity. And of course, by 'Unity' I mean an ongoing, stable awareness that there is no separate individual.

Unity happens after a sudden and spontaneous seeing into the Stillness from the Stillness that there is no separate person there. This me-subject that was there the whole life is seen as an object that is now no different than a passing thought. Again this can be described in different words, but the commonality is that through repeatedly experiencing the Silence it becomes clearer as to what is real versus what is unreal. This is refined to a point that the obvious 'pops' clearly into the pure subjectivity of what is eternally always the case. This is already being free!

From this seeing-ness you are free because the view of being separate is not a real position or perception anymore. While experiencing reality is happening, the unreal is not a possibility.

In stabilized Unity, the unreal never happens; it only appears to happen in the story. The perception of going in and out of Unity is also a story that can happen.

In a simplistic sense being separate is Unity itself believing or holding onto the idea that this object (the concept of a 'me') is the real subject. Consciousness identifies with this as though it is a separate consciousness floating around in a particular body. This is the me/mine and you/yours world that appears to the separate individual.

This is one way to describe Unity and being separate, but

again it is only another concept. In my story, the Unity glimpse has happened many times, but it has only been seen as a Unity 'experience' with more and more clarity over time. As a child I was living in Unity, yet I did not have a fully developed sense of self to appreciate the significance of this oneness. I suspect this is the same for everyone. By the time I was rooted in self/individuality I was totally lost without any hope.

In my early 20s I started looking for God as a solution to my problems. Nothing seemed to work to bring me the peace I wanted. I was looking for God on the outside, which is the only possibility for the separate individual. I went to India to see Avatars, Swamis and Yogis. The first time I went by myself and was mostly in culture shock.

When I went back a couple of years later, I was fuelled with an intense desire to know God. I threw my attention into teachings; but being innocent, I had no discernment at all. I had no way of discerning the real from unreal so I had to stumble around the block knocking on all the doors, hoping one would open up to heaven.

The more I searched, the less happy I became. I was frustrated, obsessed and desperate. I was in anguish; separate and alone in life even though I had all the things on the outside I thought I wanted.

One day I was reading a book and my mind started to expand at the thought of the infinite nature of God. I had become addicted to thinking in this way that if it was possible to comprehend God intellectually, then I would be mentally enlightened. Then a terrible pain entered my heart that I could no longer bear. I broke down and cried, "God, if you are out there please help me, I can't do this anymore."

By giving up in that moment the delicious Silence overwhelmed 'me' (and as a consequence the 'me' disappeared) and separation vanished for a brief moment. Even though it seemed brief, a second of Silence was enough to completely transform my perception and help allow what will be to be. (Perhaps this was God's way to say to my obsessively heady mind, "Shut up!") I had faith that God had heard my cry for help. I let go of trying so hard and just carried on with normal life.

It was soon after that I met a psychic at a metaphysical fair that informed me of a meditation teaching called the Bright Path. I read an article and picked up a book that resonated with what I was looking for. I wanted something that could give me peace, freedom and Joy... all the good stuff. This Teaching promised that, so I went to learn. It all sounded too good to be true, but nonetheless I was willing to give it a try.

What I loved about it was the simplicity and ease of accessing the Silence. I could repeat the techniques and experience the stillness with almost clockwork regularity. It made so much sense as a practice that I could not deny exploring it. Suddenly I had a tool that was directed to finding Unity. Of course at the time, Unity was just a concept of something that would happen in 10 years, but looking back now, the separate individual was far more out of the equation than had yet been realized. There were many glimpses of Unity on the path and the clarity increased along with the intuition of already being free.

The part that I was missing was something I could do to give focus and direction for the mind, and therefore give me the peace I wanted. For most people, that would be some form of meditation. The word meditation is a very generic word these days. 'True' meditation is an effective tool that directly leads to the Silence. The point that I would like to make is that since there is no time stamp guarantee when Unity will happen or become stabilized, we want the path to it to be not only effective but enjoyable as well. The more enjoyable it is, the more passion we will have to do it and the quicker 'popping' will happen. This is the path of joy which is a pathless path.

There is a game called "Whack a Mole" I used to play at

carnivals, and this is similar to my experiences while sitting down to meditate. The separate individual kept popping up like a mole and I kept bashing it down. Nothing I could do would keep it permanently out of the picture, but I kept whacking away. Without having an enjoyable practice I might have given up like I had many times with other pursuits.

The second time I went to India I learned a Pranayama (breathing) Technique called Vashi Yoga. Along with this tool I spent more time meditating and reading spiritual texts. Then I was overwhelmed with another glimpse of Unity that lasted for a few weeks. I think it was good timing that I was on holidays because I probably would not have been able to function very well with working a normal job and living while in drooling Bliss.

Coming back was terrifying because I had no idea how to stay in that sweet state. What could I do? Who could I ask? Eventually it vanished without a trace. Vashi Yoga could induce amazing experiences, but was not ideal or useful for integrating the spiritual into daily life. These fantastic experiences were a distraction for the ego when they were induced without readiness.

I continued to practice meditation with eyes open and eyes closed to help dissolve the stress from my nervous system. As a result, a 'new' kind of ease and peace started to become prevalent. Eventually the desire for Unity grew so strong that I made a decision to see the Teacher who taught me how to meditate. At the time he opened up a long-term meditation retreat in British Columbia.

It was wonderful to meet people from all over the world who had the same desire. The environment supported the exploration of Silence, not the story or drama. I learned what the Silence actually is besides all the ideas I had about it. I had completely undervalued it in my practice. Even though I did not see it as important, the practice I had been doing was working anyways.

The Silence was alive and had no interest in all the stuff I was continuing to make real. It used to piss me off that the Silence did not care about my drama, ggggrrrr!

Over what seemed a quick period of time I began to experience permanent peace. The separate individual would still 'pop-up' as it believed that it was the one who was on this fantastic journey. It was in competition with my fellow students to be free. Sometimes it felt like it was close and at other times far away. Then suddenly it would disappear for a week or two, and the Silence of Unity would take its place. Strangely enough, I would not realize what was going on when these glimpses happened. It makes sense now, however. 'I' had no idea, but the Teacher all of a sudden would take interest in what was happening. I would wonder why he is asking me all these questions about what I was experiencing. To me at the time I did not care because the ego had faded out of the scene, so from this perspective it was no big deal.

The relationship with the Teacher was the critical point in these glimpses of Unity. It was a pointing to that which is already free. The Teacher took responsibility for the process so that I could let it go and allow the inevitable. In my case, however, this did not happen as quickly as I would have liked. The separate individual seemed like an impossible thing to dissolve. The more I tried, the harder it seemed. Only now do I see what was happening at the time. I was taking the whole thing very seriously even though I was told repeatedly not to.

In every case it was only after the 'experiences' of Satori or Unity apparently disappeared that the mini-me would get seriously involved in the story again. "I am never going to get it, poor me," etc.

The Teacher was encouraging surrender. Surrender to the Silence, not to the Teacher as a person, or rather the surrender to the Teacher as the Silence. The magic of this relationship is in the Silence. The Teacher does not see a separate individual so the

Teaching happens spontaneously to embody the Unity that is already alive in the relationship (Pathless Path). It is sacredness beyond description. Only in hindsight can I begin to have clarity on the depth of it. Nor have I seen the end to it yet. At the time all I could do was 'be a good student' and listen. Of course I really didn't listen; I thought I was listening, but I wasn't really.

The truth is, I rarely listened which is a testament to the Teacher's eternal patience. The Teacher has committed to help the student in waking up. The student has a very simple job in listening. In my case I had the desire, but also I had tremendous arrogance. The bottom line was I wanted enlightenment as a goal because of what it would do for me. Do you see the paradox? I cannot be enlightened because I am not a separate individual in reality.

This is where a Teacher, at least in my case, was invaluable; I could not see the subtleties happening in my head. So began a relationship with the Silence and in the form of a Teacher-Student relationship with the sole purpose of Unity. Sometimes it looked like the relationship was about pouring and drinking coffee together, but it was really about Unity.

Over the few years I spent with the monks I was witness to the Teaching unfolding, yet Unity was still a mystery. I looked to the monks experiencing Unity as gods and goddesses of mysterious power. What did they do? What was their secret? I wanted some of that power!

Then something completely awful happened. My partner at the time started to be recognized as 'being free'. I was shocked. That can't be possible. Yet it was surely true as people started to come up to me every ten minutes and say, isn't she so amazing and wonderful and blah blah blah. Over and over again, it was a nightmare. I was completely jealous and frustrated by this mysterious goddess power.

What was worse was that she did not act like an enlightened woman should act! Far from it; she seemed cold and barely paid attention to me anymore. I thought enlightened people would be more loving! Later I was told that she had her attention on the Silence instead of 'me', but still, how rude is that! What about my 'me' doesn't deserve love and attention?

I felt trapped in a relationship with a wall, a wall of stillness, but still a wall nonetheless. No longer did I have the same safety and comfort that you would want in a loving relationship. I was terribly exposed. All my fears of being rejected and abandoned came roaring in. No longer could I hide. Now I had no choice, either run away screaming or get enlightened. I could not keep living like a trapped rat. The ego was squirming.

Looking back I see how perfect the situation was, because it caused me to reevaluate what I wanted. Before that, I would have bet my life that I wanted freedom, but it really put that to the test. Actually what I saw was that I wanted the perfect relationship more than Freedom. After awhile of fighting internally and squirming with jealousy, I decide to use the situation to my advantage. She became like a mini-teacher for me. Mini because she was actually quite tiny. I began to observe her (like a scientist) to see what an enlightened woman is really like. When we were in Puerto Rico she cried because her father was in pain. I thought, "She cannot be enlightened, she is crying." Another concept I had to face, the idea that Unity was an emotionless Bliss.

I just kept observing her hoping to find the secret.

"What do I do?" I'd say.

"Just be effortlessly still, you are trying too hard," she'd reply.

"Jesus whatever!!"

I kept trying to figure it out by analyzing the experience I was going through.

In Mexico I made a huge discovery all by 'myself'; I was reading the Upanishads and for some reason that pain in the heart had returned like it had so many years ago. I was frustrated and tired of trying, so I said in my head, "You know what, I am just going to be effortless still and stop trying so hard for two weeks." That was 'my' idea not hers... wink-wink. I will not care about my experience for two weeks and just explore the stillness. Trying to get enlightened was becoming way too exhausting. Simultaneously and spontaneously to this was an energetic relief. It was as if the struggle and trying died.

Then the most amazing thing happened, I started to enjoy life without the usual commentary and trying to get it. More accurately, I had the usual commentary, but didn't care anymore. When I returned from Mexico to Canada, I had shared the experience with my Teacher and the students. I was encouraged to keep sharing and exploring that.

For the next year or so I was working with a guy who was building a custom home near the retreat center. During the day I worked there and at night came to the retreat to listen and share with the Teachers and students.

I could say that this year was the year of stabilization although that stable part never really stops 'becoming stable' in my opinion. It's as if stability is infinite, more rock-like now than a second ago. Lighter than air now.

There were many moments of clarity and recognition of there being only Unity as the path disappeared. Each time it was like seeing for the first time. Reality was unraveling. I still had concepts that I could not see, which was the great benefit of having guidance from a master of the mind who could see through them all. I would continually 'share' in group discussions to get a reflection back about what I was experiencing. The main block that I could not see was that because I had not been told, "Yes you are free," I believed I was missing something that I needed to figure out. You would think that I could see that, but the voice was hidden because I thought that voice was 'me'. One day I was questioning something when the Teacher stopped me mid-sentence and said, "You are still trying to figure it out." "Bing-bing," the lights went on and I saw that. I saw that I still believed I thought that I was missing something and needed to figure out what that something was. I saw it (the thought – not the something that I was missing) and that was it; I have never needed to figure anything out since then. Whew! What a relief! After thousands of years of thinking and being in my head, I can finally relax!

These moments were like little chinks in the armor of believing in a separate 'I' or 'me'.

Then came the problem of being acknowledged in Unity. How was I to know I am free unless I am told by an outside authority? Waiting for those wonderful words, "You did it, you are free," then they hand you the certificate of Unification for you to proudly display on the wall. The trumpets blare and Jesus gives you the wink and the gun.

The truth is, you are already free and all that needs to happen is the seeing of it. Once it is seen clearly the desire to stay there in the bliss of Unity outweighs any desire for acknowledgment or attention of any kind. In other words there is no need to wait, yet apparently we do anyway.

The separate individual is waiting to live up to its concept of Unity or to be hit with the beam of truth. A more dangerous problem, however, is actually thinking you are in Unity. It becomes very easy for the mind to think it is in Unity because of the Unity experience. A Unity experience is not Unity because it is owned by the 'you' center. Once it happens it is gone.

In my own experience, even after seeing there is no separation the mind kept popping up again in subtle ways. Without guidance, I am not sure what would have happened. Would it have taken longer? Would I have become an enlightened spiritual ego? Maybe I could have become rich and famous. Who knows?

One thing is for sure, I am suspicious of people who have not 'done the work' with or without a teacher and claim that they are free. I am not saying that it cannot happen, but that it is very easy to claim Unity as an object to own. Also without a teacher that has walked far ahead on the path it is easy to settle for less. Unity is infinite, so there is always more. This is the humility that is an invitation to continually surrender to the infinity of Unity. The ego would rather do it on its own – and believe me I tried very hard to do just that. I wanted to do it by myself.

It is very difficult to see a false teacher (actually impossible) without a clear awareness of the Silence. I have been in this situation a number of times; there have been many famous teachers who I personally believe are not free, but this does not dismiss their role or place in the spiritual community. They are dynamic personalities, yes. They can speak the truth, yes. We can be attracted to these personalities, yes. Armed with words of truth, they are very attractive. The concept of truth has become like the McDonald's of spirituality these days, or the fast food of enlightenment. Enlightenment is not made of cardboard, however. It is natural and organic. No offense intended to McDonald's; I hope I don't get sued for this comparison.

The fact that I have spent time with 'false teachers' is not a bad thing. Not everyone needs to do this, but in my case it helped me see what I truly wanted. It was a painful time in my life. I was not a victim, however, I chose it – literally. It helped me be honest and see that what I wanted more than anything was to go back to the innocence and peace I glimpsed in my meditation course. I used to talk about spiritual stuff with people, but after thousands of "I know, I know, I knows" I stopped talking about it. Everyone knows because they heard it at McDonald's. They read about it at the dentist or they saw it on Oprah.

Everyone is an expert, but no one knows what she or he is talking about because it is all just a lovely idea. This is why the truth as a concept is dangerous to the sincere seeker. This is why I say that everything here is a concept. Never hold onto what I say because it is not true; it is only a representation. Nobody can give you this truth because you 'are' it already.

Without a clear experience of the Silence, it is very difficult to see through all the distractions and teachings. A sincere seeker need not worry because as intuition gets refined through practice and grace (sometimes by being burned), the obvious cuts through the endless dead ends and mind traps. From the perspective of Unity, this is a miracle that has nothing to do with 'me'. It makes me happy that I do not need to convince anybody of anything anymore. I know that there are no accidents on the path; and if someone needs to spend 20 years on some weird and strange journey, who am I to be so arrogant to say that they are off the path? From Unity's perspective, nobody has ever been off the path. As my Teacher says, "Everyone is exactly where they need to be right now." Of course if where you are sucks, well then, stay open to another possibility.

I know that to the individual who is in a cult, or stuck in painful therapies for no reason, that I would be very selfish if I did not say, "Hey you don't have to take that route, check this one out!" It is every human's right to take the 'wrong' or 'long' path. It does not matter from the pathless Unity perspective; it only matters to you and your 'mini-me' that experiences the pain or joy of your choices. So choose wisely!

At a certain point in my life I had to stand up to my father and say, "Look I am tired of you telling me which way to go in my life. I know you are doing it because you love me, but I want the freedom to do the wrong thing." It was important for me to see for myself, develop the intuition and follow my bliss. Did I choose correctly or ideally most of the time? Nope.

The desire to see for real is sufficient and each so-called trap is just a humorous stepping stone into a clearer view of what is. As long as we don't get stuck there forever, it is movement along the path. All that being said, if I would have listened to the universe as it told me in plain English through many different people, "DO NOT GO THERE!" I would have not burned myself so badly; but then again, I would not have learned what I do not want.

One thing I was told was that freedom takes boldness. The last thing I was holding onto was the experience of Unity itself. It was like my own private secret. I considered it arrogant to talk about it or claim it in any way. Who could claim 'all there is' anyway? It was much more comfortable for me to just sit back and enjoy it for myself. This was the arrogance. Yet what I could not see at the time was that I was not fully free. I had settled for a kind of personal Unity experience where a little bit of me was going along for the ride. I did not want to give my special Unity away, but keep it all to myself and in a sense retire from life after 'getting it'. In my case I needed to be bold. As an introvert and a polite Canadian, I did not want to make a big deal out of something that in essence was 'just what we all are anyway'. This is how the separate individual will rationalize separation right up to the end.

My Teacher says, "One percent of the ego is still all of it in play." Now I had a new problem, how could I step out, be bold, and share the indescribable?

I started to try. It was brutal, but nonetheless I kept trying to be bold and come out of the Unity closet. I had an idea or script in my head of how I wanted to share it and it always came out completely different. This was frustrating, to say the least.

A friend named Narain came to me after one of those brutal moments of sharing 'my' Unity and said, "You will be free when you no longer care about being acknowledged."

Then over the next few months something miraculous started to happen. I fell into an innocence of play. The Silence became so enjoyable that I lost all interest in what I thought about myself or Unity. I lost all interest in what others thought about me or my experience. I even lost interest in what my Teacher thought. Everything became about enjoying the Silence. There was only the completeness of 'THIS' (Unity).

Then I started to share just for the love of it, forgetting about how it looked. Ironically I became the most comfortable with being 'me' I had ever been.

Then there was boldness, but not the boldness of a separate individual, but the boldness of all there is. This is the obviousness of Unity. There was nothing to prove but a natural cosmic oomph to give it all away since it does not belong to anyone specifically anyway. No longer was I afraid to look arrogant, but was willing to simply put forth the truth of what is as it is.

This is important since enlightenment is often seen as a mystical thing that happens to the few special ones. When it happens to that guy or that girl, and the 'no way, not him, are you joking', then it becomes something more tangible. By sharing it, it becomes obvious that this is the underlying reality and sameness of every 'one'.

This was, however, not the moment I became free (an important distinction); I have always been free since all there is is Unity. This is seeing in innocence without a separate individual. There never was a separate individual who suffered in ignorance. In terms of linear time, I had been in and out of Unity for a long time before that point. The Teacher was waiting for it to stabilize, or not. To be clear, stabilized Unity happens by enjoying the Silence and being content there! Holding Nothing! Taking nothing seriously! All of this happened effortlessly without 'me' trying. When I noticed the trying – I stopped. How much effort does it take to be what you already are? Unity is effortless and pathless.

To some of the students, I had achieved something that they wanted yet only the ego can achieve something. I had lost something. I was not trying to be humble by saying that I did not do anything, like accepting an Oscar: "I could not have done it without Buddha, I would like to thank my mother who believed that I could do it, I would like to thank the enlightened, etc..."

I had always perceived that Unity was the end of the search, but it is only the beginning. I was in for a shock because the real work would now begin. I would see what Unity is like in truth, not based on what I had read or heard but based on this ever-unfolding perspective. In other words, I had no idea what Unity was or is or will be. I still don't get it, I just write books about it for fun and because it is apparently what I do.

Life naturally gives us the next thing we need to let go of. Surrender becomes automatic because life is seen as it is. It is not own-able. In Unity nothing is held onto because it is recognized that life is only flowing by. The possibility exists, however, to take what comes seriously. This is the fall from grace. This is unlikely for those who have mastered surrender and/or who have guidance. Even today I can expect a slap in the back of the head if 'I am off' or I take things seriously. My Teacher will never hesitate to point out when my focus becomes about me. This is what I hired him for, otherwise I would have picked up a book at the local New Age shop and asked it to be my Teacher. The book cannot smack me (lovingly, not super hard) when I lose focus. I wish I could smack you (in a cute way), but that is a physical impossibility according to our current understanding of physics.

Divine Intelligence reveals that there is nothing to be gained by holding onto anything. This is worth repeating: there is nothing to be gained by holding onto anything. The only thing that can be gained is a sense of being separate, which seems like a choice, but at a certain point in consciousness it would be a ridiculous choice. The insight into the unreality of what we call separation continues in Unity. This is something that cannot be understood but intuited. I am still discovering what the heck an ego even is, but I am not alone; even the experts have millions of definitions. By dissolving into Unity, the only conclusion I can say for sure is that it does not exist. As an appearance, however, I do find it fascinating – like watching a beautifully colored fish swim in an aquarium.

I am not beyond guidance at this point because I am not

finished. Whether it is you, my Teacher or a tree, there is only receptivity to all there is (except for my boss at work, I don't care what he thinks). The revelation of Unity is an eternal one. Unity is seamlessly revealing what it is. The good news is that without a separate individual revealing this, it is effortless. Insight has happened over the course of the last few years and I have no reason to think it will not continue to happen. After all, they say this Unity is Infinite so why would it come to an end? Can you imagine Jesus or Buddha giving you a button and a ribbon that says, "You did it, this is it"? Then life would be completely boring. The fact is that Unity is like being a newborn explorer; everything is fresh, alive and awesome. Even the drama is awesome, since you are not involved in it. Like watching someone slip and fall on the ice, you know it hurts but you can't help but laugh. How rude, no?

It is all about where attention settles effortlessly and without manipulation. What is important determines where our attention goes. I wish I could have told you that all the problems I experience disappeared, but they did not; in some ways they became worse. Financially, romantically and socially things got worse. What disappeared or what I lost was the suffering over them. I no longer suffered at the challenges of life and 'fate'; and as a result, my experience of life transformed. My character in the world looks exactly the same and has the same tendencies (for the most part).

An incredible trust in what happens took over. It suggested that as long as I continued to surrender to God, life would get better. This has been my experience. The result never looks like I think it is going to, but it is always better. The less it is about 'me', the better. The less 'I' think the better. To this day I have problems, challenges, such as relationship, work, and money, but they are not personal. I do not think of them since they always resolve themselves with simplicity. I have an intellect that gets used, but it no longer uses me. I have emotions that come and go, but I'm no longer attached to owning them.

This is the perception of 'my story'; but like I said, it can change. No story is absolutely true. If every human 'popped' into Unity, we would each have a unique story to tell. The only common thread would be of the Silence. Regardless of the perception is all comes back to the Silence.

After Unity

There may be a period of time in which we are walking on a cloud of bliss unmoved by the world's challenges. The full glory of awakening takes all of our attention. How this is lived may be somewhat unique depending on the mind/body/energetic system of the sage, but the transcendent nature of Unity eclipses all our humanness. Or so it seems.

This seems like a wonderful period in which there is a clear seeing into the Unity of all there is and in the disappearance of a separate individual there is an indescribable delight. This is literally like being reborn in innocence again. Suddenly we are playing in Heaven. The reality, however, is that staying in this exalted state for a long time is usually not possible. Even though most of us would just love to hang out in this bliss cloud, forever drooling, God has other plans. Most people come down off the cloud and the human part of life starts to reveal and integrate itself to this new way of being. "What? I have to go to work if I am enlightened, that is so not cool!"

However, this too is a very exciting realization, but can also bring up some confusion and doubts for those who experience it. Being around like-minded people certainly helps, but often to find someone to relate to this in the average city can be rare. For those in smaller communities – good luck! If you do know people who don't take things seriously, even if they aren't very enlightened, in your opinion, cling to them. If they don't take you and your enlightenment seriously, they are your new best friends. God has sent that person to you so you can lighten up and relax.

The doubts after Unity can be of the nature of, "How can I be in Unity if I am experiencing this or that?" Now we get to see the truth of Unity, not the concepts we held in the mind. Seeing that there is only Unity is just the beginning. This is the natural state of being human.

Before Unity, in some way we were resisting what is. There was not a full allowing of all experiences to come and go without grabbing, judging and comparing them. There is a very common-sense notion that 'in Unity' there will be no more thoughts, emotions and certainly no more ego after Unity. The separate individual is hoping for this. The separate ego thinks it can know what freedom is like. Since the separate ego is a bunch of concepts, these concepts can still put up a fight for control – only apparently. After Unity the concepts come without the separation, although it is possible to re-identify with them to magically re-create separation again. This is the incredible power 'you' have. 'You' have the power to fall asleep again. The good news is that this dance is usually very clear at this point in Unity, especially if you have a valid meditation practice.

At this point we can see the value in 'doing the work' or 'walking the path' versus a random popping. You are now so familiar with the Silence and popping in and out that you know all the tricks in the book. You are a master of the mind. Whatever it throws up is irrelevant to the indescribable obviousness of all there is!

It is assumed that upon awakening you never again have to worry about your ego. In one sense, that is very true, but being aware of your attention is important. This is even more important than before because the mind gets subtler, and freedom means freedom to think or do anything – including falling asleep again as well. There are no rules or judgments anymore. All is allowed. This is the double-edged sword one discovers after a more stable Unity appears. What I have observed in others and myself is a tendency to get lazy with self-observation. Just because there is no longer a separate observer does not mean that observation becomes useless. There can be a relaxation or so little of the sense of separation that a subtle arrogance of 'being beyond and above' can creep in. Watch for this little devil!

If Unity has become stable enough, the humility of the Silence will just laugh at it. If not it can lead to an 'enlightened' ego. This is the part of the manual that most seekers forget to read. It is in small print next to the section called, "Be careful what you wish for!"

Freedom is not just a cool thing you do to impress your friends. It is impossible to fool God or Buddha! Once you start on this path, it is a permanent deal. This is why I keep coming back to a path of joy. Since you are going to be on it forever you might as well get comfy and enjoy it. By enjoying it that doesn't mean that shit doesn't still come up! Believe me, unless you are a robot or no longer breathing, you will have all sorts of things which come up for you to be allowed. Never take it seriously and keep on walking.

Unity is eternal. Therefore to give up and be lazy like you achieved something is the separate person resurrecting itself again. Unity is not a retirement plan, but getting the best job you have ever had. During the absolute oneness of Unity without any movement there is a total freedom and invincibility. What happens when all programming, conditioning and all the human drama come rushing back to you after Unity? The thought can be, "I thought I let all of this go!" Then perhaps you try to keep Unity there as an object, as the fear of losing the precious experience comes up.

All of these experiences are totally natural and are a deeper insight into the reality of what it really means to 'BE FREE'. You could say the process of stabilization is ongoing in that there is always potential for a clearer perception of all that is and clarity on the functioning of manifestation. This is the wonder of God. The end result to all of this continued surrender is a deep love and humility that trumps all prior experiences. All experience – no matter how bad or wonderful – come and go, but you do not. This is the Unification on a deeper level of a self that can allow the most limited experiences because they too are a part of manifestation and natural functioning.

As long as we hold onto anything at all, even if we are unaware of it, we are not truly free in the ultimate sense. Perhaps this is what sages are referring to when saying that I am not free until all humanity is free. There is certainly truth in this statement. The greatest of sages having seen deeply enough into the absolute and letting go of the tiniest scrap of limitation have only one thing left to do. That is to serve the poor little buggers that still believe they are separate.

Being in Unity is not just transcendent but more importantly immanent. It is the separate individual that looks to hide in the transcendent quality of Unity, but this is not the whole truth of it. After Unity is reached, there is an ongoing opening into the fullness of what real life is like. Nobody actually knows what real life is like because it does not happen to a separate person. It is an all-inclusive and immanent deepening of Unity as it is ever revealing. This is the ultimate mystery.

In this way of being there can be no control over events that happen. This means to wish for only bliss instead of pain is a bitter joke. Instead there is a resting in the bliss of all there is in which anything can and does happen. That being said, through surrender and the stabilizing of Unity, bliss and peace are the consistent 'experience' one has in general. This is so because by holding nothing, what is left is the fullness of God that is unmoving bliss.

After Unity emotions will arise, but they are largely unattached energies that come and go. The difference between that and a separate individual is that the individual thinks that anger happens to me. In the sage, the energy 'labeled' anger comes and goes without a personalization or attachment to it. There is nothing personal anymore that needs to hold onto objects. From the outside someone could say she was angry, but that is not what happened from the sage's perspective.

The hysterical thing is that this is also the truth of what is before Unity. The same energy of anger comes up. It comes up for no one. It too comes and goes, to be expressed by what I perceive as 'me' or you have come to think of as 'you'. Then what happens is the separate individual grabs it, labels it as 'anger' and says, "Mine." 'Me angry, you angry' is a product of the old brain we inherited from our ancestors. All there is, however, is Unity. The grabbing of this energy is just another part of the story of awakening as it unfolds before and after.

After Unity, it is not so much the story disappearing as the amazing ability to SEE straight though it – even as the scenes of life are playing out. This is how the sage can relax and enjoy life. She or he will enjoy it not because they are disconnected or detached; quite the opposite. Now they are fully engaged in everything and getting their hands dirty. It is the freedom to allow the natural events to unfold in the story without the incessant need of the ego to manipulate it.

After Unity, it is clearly seen that the separate individuals are only apparently separate and have no actual substance. It becomes easier and easier to see through the individual story to the Unity that is there. The separate individual is no more real than a chair or anything else. It is a part of the totality of creation happening now. That is all.

Separation appears to happen within the absolute Unity of all there is. After Unity the fresh and new perspective unfolds forever as the 'Great Divine Adventure'. The personality and/or the uniqueness of our essence is what makes us human and is now capable of being fully loved. The capacity to love our 'self' and our humanness has reached an infinite potential. As an extension of this, 'love thy neighbor' becomes absolute. It is this joy of the one in Unity to continue to surrender the attraction to conceptualize which separates as life, experiences, people and events are now seen as an expression of Unity itself. Life is no longer about your 'you'. How freeing and wonderful is that? Now you can live for the rest of humanity in service of their divinity.

You are the example of the freedom of Unity – don't ruin it by thinking again!

Extraordinary Ordinariness

The wonder of Unity is that even the most ordinary experiences like stretching or picking your nose can become superbly amazing. The fact that there is even existence is a celebration. You are existence as it is! You are alive! Is this not a miracle of all miracles? You could have not existed, but you do!

This is the only thing worth thinking about (besides Silence and snacks). Think about the amazing-ness that you have popped into THIS – right here – right now! I know, maybe the world you perceive is not the greatest place to be, but forget about the world 'out there' for a moment. What about just here? Right here is the space, the breath and the Silence. The space, breath and the Silence are the capacity for all that is happening in the room. In other words you are ALIVE. Let's go and celebrate! You are breathing! Awesome! You did it, that is all you have to do, just keep doing that and you will be fine.

Breathing is amazing, touching objects and feeling their texture and shape is incredible. Hearing the cars go by is a joyful orchestra of sounds. The little things in life are now the grandest of all. Disneyland and Vegas have nothing on this extraordinary ordinariness. This is heaven.

In general, the simple little fact of you existing goes on completely unappreciated. We have been trained to seek outside ourselves for happiness. Some seek material things, but you know the drill there. The seeker seeking happiness is exactly the same. Seeking the extraordinary outside is a great way to avoid what we already have and are. It is not found 'out there' in the world. Nobody can give it to you because you already have it.

Unity is the clear seeing that the extraordinary is in what is obvious and simple as well as jumping off a cliff and pulling your parachute with one second to spare. This is the beauty of what is. It is the removal of the conceptual framework that keeps saying, "Boring, old." This is the structure that seems to happen in life whereby there is a missing piece always in the back of the head. To seek period means that there is a perception that something must be missing. What is missing is only the seeing of what you already are. Your life has always been extraordinary, you just didn't see it. It has nothing to do with the activities you do or the epiphanies you receive.

This stimulates the interest in taking drugs to escape from reality for some. I got caught in this cycle in my early 20s. I was looking for the extraordinary; a way for something to come close to my concept of what heaven is like. I had built up a divine concept and my life was nothing compared to it. How could it be?

I started taking magic mushrooms to open the door to something more fantastic. The only problem was, the door would not stay open, and as I continued on my 'normal' life just looked more and more dull and uninteresting in comparison with the 'high' of this magical world. I became addicted to the spiritual experiences of being high – or at least they appeared to be spiritual at the time.

What am I supposed to do now? Do I keep taking them forever? It became clear that continuing to use the mushrooms was not the solution. It just kept making my life seem more and more dull. How can I get high without them? Then I saw clearly what I wanted. I knew that certain aspects of my trip were more real (at the time) than my ordinary life. These experiences such as the sense of time disappearing or seeing that everything is alive and breathing were common in this magical world. Also, however, I knew that I had created them artificially by forcing these experiences. I did something chemically to my brain to open a door.

The apparent reality of these experiences convinced me that I could experience them naturally. The solution appeared simple – let's get enlightened so that I can fly around with the angels 24 hours a day! I wanted to have the extraordinary fill up the ordinary.

After dabbling in some strange teachings here and there, I began to see the value of meditation. Research had shown that certain chemicals that induced the spiritual high are naturally present in the blood. Also these chemicals are released from the brain during certain meditation practices. DMT is one such chemical present in humans, plants and animals. An interesting fact is that, structurally, it is also one of the simplest molecules on earth.

Of course meditation is a very generic term that could mean thousands of things for different people. I wish I could come up with a word that was better, but I haven't so far. Ascension is a nice word because it means to rise above, but that also has a New Age connotation. By ascending we rise beyond the limitations and programming of the mind. This is a natural way to continually let go and allow the aliveness of joy within to take flight in our nervous system.

Meditation is the "Cosmic oomph of exploring the Silence as it is." How about that? Meditation is both extraordinary and ordinary. Ordinary and extraordinary qualities of meditation are: Stillness, thoughts, energy, nothing, sensations, feelings, peace, quiet, awareness, Silence, nothingness, expansion, Presence, fullness, emotions, eternal, infinite, empty, thinking, nothing happening, movement, impersonal, personal, allowing, all that is, contentment, Love and Bliss, inclusive, transcendent, nondual, phenomena, subjectivity, oneness, Self, no-self, Unity.

Meditation is the most important practice to realize the truth, awaken and get happy. Unless you get lucky, struck by the spiritual beam, you need to make a regular practice of it. The more familiar we become with being in the Silence the more permanent it fills up our lives until we are bathing in joy 24/7. Eventually nothing shakes our focus off this delightful oneness, not even cheesecake. The culmination of the regular practice of meditation, eyes open and eyes closed manifests the union of the extraordinary with the ordinary. This extraordinary ordinariness is a 'high'-light of UNITY.

The Land of Pause

The land of pause is a wonderful place of mystery. To enter it is to enter the unknown where anything can happen. Can you imagine what it would be like to just stop things for a moment to 'get a grip' on the situation or to have a 'reality check'?

Welcome to the land of pause! That is exactly what we can do here. Anytime we feel overloaded, mentally or emotionally, or feel like exploding with anxiety or bliss, as anxiety is in truth bliss experienced through the filter of separation, we can remember where we are. The Silence is the gateway to this land of pausing. Her cousin is the 'reset button', a similar way to come back to clarity.

Pause has been around forever and has been referred to by different names. Some call her holy spirit, the miracle of 'now'. Usually this moment of pause has come completely by coincidence in the past when all of a sudden we were gifted with a little break from our tired lives. The secret to pause access is to simply appreciate it more than thinking. Now you can be aware of this little break when awareness rushes in and says, "Stop for a second, relax, and be alert."

A different choice is made available, such as to see where we have been caught up in seriousness of mental dialogue. Pause can have many different results, but all of them are super great when compared to the alternative. Maybe you get an insight or are suddenly more easily able to allow the things we are faced with throughout the day, who knows? The key is to thank the queen of pause for sending this awareness to you.

Through praise and gratitude the land of pause comes even before we think we need it and life just gets a lot easier. Sometimes there is just a 'glitch in the Matrix', and we get stuck in a loop inside our head. Maybe this happens more than we would like to admit. Okay I admit, it has happened to me on occasion.

Before you freak out, just stop; breathe. Start over again. After all, you have eternity, so what is your rush? Take a moment to see clearly what it is you want more than anything right now.

What do I want? What am I grateful for? And what can I praise? Also work to attract pause.

"Peace and freedom," you may say. Okay then, stay here in the land of pause at least for awhile until you are so clear you can go about your busy-business again without worry. Don't worry if things get too much again, just tap your head three times and say to yourself, "There is no place like pause. There is no place like pause. There is no place like pause."

By pausing we realign ourselves with the easiness of Silence.

Pause is a straight up gift from the universe (or God). You don't have to go looking for it when you are overwhelmed because by sheer cosmic oomph it will open up or 'give you the time of day'. All you have to do is take advantage of it. Life until now for most of us is spent avoiding this invitation from the Queen of Pause.

Pause is called "the holy instant" in *A Course in Miracles*. It is the sudden gift of awareness. You did not choose to become aware, but out of the blue it arrives. It is only up to you to accept it, see it or to deny it. Almost everyone denies it because they love stress and drama more than the peace of pause. Also they are simply not aware of the land of pause due to the effort of incessant denial. Now that I have told you about pause, there are no more excuses for you.

Pause responds to your attention and love. The more you enjoy the peace and have that as a priority, the more the pause will come into your life. The 'attitude of gratitude' will strengthen this gift immensely and enliven the Silence. Eventually the opportunity to continually live in the presence of GOD by being aware of the Silence will be an easy choice. Until then, however, keep pausing.

This is Awe-Full

The other day I was out for a walk and was crossing the street when a car ran a red light and almost hit me. I have watched a lot of movies and I have envisioned myself in this situation in my head. I see myself jumping and doing a flip over the car. Now I know for sure that that is not what I do. Instead I freeze.

I put my arms up and like a deer in the headlights, I froze. I am not proud of this response, but that seems to be what I do when I am faced with sudden death. I wish I could have told you that I jumped over the car like a ninja! That would be sweet!

This response happened to me before whenever I've been shocked by loud noises or bright lights. The nervous system goes into a stunned state of 'OMG'.

In a similar way, Unity or standing in the presence of God is a kind of shock to the nervous system. I don't mean in an awful sense like an electrical shock but in an 'awe-full' stunning of presentation of brightness. Not the brightness of intense white light but the brightness of awe and wonder. This is the sign of heaven. It is like we are all escaping from jail and they've got this big spotlight up there that angels are waving around and if it hits you there is nothing to do but freeze and be caught up in this beauty of surrendering. This divine light is what makes Unity so simple and natural. It is effortless because it is intensely engaging. It is effortless because it is 'home'.

Have you ever observed how flies and moths are attracted to the light? I used to marvel at their stupidity. What are you doing? You are going nowhere! They are helpless because of that light and so are we – especially if we have been bitten by the Unity bug – so to speak. Once that light gets switched on, we have no choice but to keep buzzing around it.

Imagine for a moment that there is a home which you have never left. How much effort would it take to see it? Imagine that all the effort of your entire life was only to distract you from seeing your home and where you are already. The seeing of this is awe. WOW!

I am not saying that effort to become free is a waste of time. Of course all we can do is put effort into it and work on becoming free especially in the beginning. The more you put into it, the more you get from it, or so it seems. I understand that it looks that way and perhaps there is no other option.

The mind is not used to searching for the light, let alone staying there. All the effort is required only to see it, but once the Silence is seen clearly – usually with additional guidance – effort becomes less necessary with the increased awareness of Silence.

The struggle or hard part is to find it. The intellect has done its job. The intelligent moth has now found the light bulb and can become a happy stupid moth.

When the Silence is permanently in the awareness, then effort is no longer required. Unity is integrated and stabilized with absolute effortlessness. The power of awe does all of the work. I know, I know this is awe-full, but what are you gonna do?

Without 'You' There

The flow and ease of Unity happens because without you there, there is no obstacle to what is already free flowing, natural or spontaneous. This does not mean that in Unity what is free flowing looks like perfection. Unity does not match what the mind thinks is pretty or nice. The idea that things that happen in Unity are only sweet and nice is a production of the mind's idealist projection of enlightenment or heaven. Sometimes things look nice when they align with our preference, and then sometimes they look bad when what happens is not our preference. What happens has nothing to do with Unity or with you personally. A separate individual cannot help but think in this dualistic way since it is structured in subject/object duality.

This projection can be dangerous for the seeker of enlightenment, since by its very definition an ideal can never be attained. It is called ideal because it never happens. This keeps the bunny hopping and hoping for the carrot forever. At a certain point the seeker may give up because they get fed up with chasing the carrot. This could be a re-engaging of the ego or a precursor to freedom. Who knows?

Two types of giving up

The first type of giving up happens when the seeker stops seeking freedom and decides to seek happiness in the world. This can strengthen the illusion of the separate individual. Ironically this can look like a greater freedom since the ego is free from seeking enlightenment, but this does not change the fact that there is still the identity in separation and seeking, albeit a different objective than freedom.

The second type of giving up is when there is a genuine desire to give up the struggle. The seeker still wants freedom more than anything, but they are so sick of trying so hard that they pause.

In that moment of pause there is a possibility that a path of joy might take over the process effortlessly. Without the ideal 'maker' – the little you – what 'is' is perfection because it is seen in the infinite light of Unity. The ease and flow of this separate you not being there is the perfection, not some ideal state, in which the mind lives with an idea of perfection.

The divine rule is that whatever you think of as heaven, it is greater. So coming up with the greatest conceptual heaven is seen as a waste of time because that is not it. If you follow this to the end of time, the mind must get bored with this conceptualizing and realizes its own limitation. When this happens the mind and separate 'you' collapse – even if just for an instant – and there is freedom from you and your mind.

Simply put, effort is there as long as you identify with being a separate individual. This is okay and cannot be any other way. There is no need to change this by trying to be effortless because that is only the separate individual effort-ing to stop effort. Now you can laugh because it is all really crazy, what can you do?

Since the separate individual lives in duality you can do reverse psychology on the universe to trick the fabric of space-time. Just try the opposite to confuse the mind for a second. If you have been trying to stop trying, instead of trying to stop, try trying even harder to try. This confuses the mind because it goes against the laws of common sense. Why would you do that? This is the point; you wouldn't do that! You then disappear into the Silence because the laws of separate dualistic thinking seem to vanish. If you want to stop thinking and trying to stop won't work, try thinking as much as you possibly can in that moment. Think with as much effort as you can right now with the greatest amount of effort. See and explore how crazy everything including your mind is and have fun doing it. We live in crazy-land inside our heads, but those crazy rules don't apply without you there!

Without you there it gets easier... so try harder, think more and get frustrated so you can get out of the way quicker and see that, in truth, 'nothing' is in the way. Wink, wink, nudge, nudge.

The Absence of the Presense of Presence or Absence

As noted earlier, sometimes it is useful to confuse or shock the mind into submission. This can induce awe. Of course you can just tell it to shut up and see if it listens; that is great as well, but usually not very effective. We have no control over when this will happen, but this is an agenda of the spiritual seeker for sure. This seeker is smart enough to realize at a certain point that when the mind does shut up there is peace.

Of course it can only reference this as a past memory. "Oh that was such a peaceful experience." This is because the seeker disappears in the moment that there is no separation. It's a popping game.

This is the purpose of the Zen koan or the whacking of the student on the head. Please don't hit me unless you can guarantee I will wake up! The Zen koan could be something like, "When the chicken is dancing in the falling cloud the singing frog bounces on a waterfall of trees... ice cream melting." I think it is pretty clear what that means, so I won't go into explaining it. (I have no idea what that means.)

At certain points in my life, falling into the unknown would happen when I was thinking about a spiritual truth or concept that was beyond my experience. One time I experienced this while in India. I had discovered a book called *Amritanubhava* or *Experience of Immortality* by Ramesh Balsekar, originally written by the Indian saint Jnaneshvara who lived from 1130 to 1183 AD.

The material was apparently way beyond my 'level' of consciousness at the time. It was describing non-duality through poetic verses such as "sweetness is inseparable from sugar". Not only was the poetry beyond my ability to grasp, but the commentary was also beyond me in two different ways. The first was the description of non-duality and the second was the actual wording. Such as the title of this chapter, it confused me no matter how many times I read it.

The basic idea that Jnaneshvara is expressing is that the absolute and the relative are one. The unmanifest/manifest, subject/object, consciousness/appearance, self/no-self, Shiva/Shakti, Christ/holy spirit, infinite/finite, nothingness/everythingness are not two but one and the same. The ocean and the waves are the same. The waves are the appearance of the ocean 'waving'.

Now, it may seem from a certain point of view that I was wasting my time; but interestingly, looking back I see that I had a 'double' Unity whammy hit on the head. The resonance with Unity pointed out by the 'Saint' and the 'author' was very strong. The confusion of my mind with the wording as well as the intellectual understanding was a blessing. The text actually was proving to demonstrate what the "experience of immortality" was all about. It was quite literally "beyond the mind". The fact was that I didn't even need to understand it at all because that which is real is sufficient and intuitively known. Obviously both the author and the original writer coming from the intention to share Unity through this medium was enough to shake things up.

As the confusion became greater, my heart began to sing with a rush of joy. Then a moment came where the joy became so intense and the confusion in my head overwhelming – my eyes likely started to cross – Unity burst open and all there 'was' was an eternity of laughter. I was overwhelmed with still, unmoving bliss. This Unity glimpse did not last long, however, but was more impactful than I would realize for many years.

This was not the first time I would be introduced to this secret Zen technique. The universe seemed to love to confuse me whenever I would get too heady. I guess that is what happens when your mission in life is to figure it all out.

On one occasion at a retreat I was so stuck in my head, I could not stop thinking. No matter what advice I got I simply could not cease the chatter. At a retreat I was surrounded by monks who were helpless to change my mind. At one point they had even assigned the guy they called Indra to "get it done". He was like an enforcer in the mafia, but in a good way. He was to "be my mirror". A mirror is someone to be with you, literally every second of every day, not just to annoy you, but to help you get over your 'stuff'.

I was very stubborn and refused help and stayed isolated in my self-absorption. I was in my own little world, with a big sign saying, "Stay the heck out!"

Then one day my Teacher came over and threw a massive old book – thousands of years old – called *Vasistha's Yoga* by Swami Venkatesananda in front of me. He said, "I want you to read 50 pages a day. This should burn some brain cells."

So I began to read it and in a similar way I had no idea what I was reading, but because of the resonance with the energy or intention of Unity coming through the material, the mind started to still on its own. It fascinated me that something so old seemed so current and alive as if the original author was sitting in front of me. The book's message is repeated throughout by stories, descriptions and analogies. In every possible way, the author tries to hit you on the head with infinite consciousness. This is useful for someone like me who thinks a lot. It basically says... all there is is infinite consciousness and anything else is like a thought floating and/or appearing within/on that. It burns brain cells in that it hits you with this theme through stories of Unity that the mind can't wrap itself around. Hence all the mind can do is 'burn up'.

The teaching repeatedly says the same thing. You can sum up all of the thousands of great works and the words of all the thousands of sages throughout all space and time. You sum it up with the words: 'Be still'.

Of course the words 'be still' didn't do it, so I kept reading, but it is always useful to summarize what the heck all of us are doing within this spiritual quest. I am still amazed that when the 'pause' comes to me I am reminded of the simplicity of, "It is only about the Silence... period."

Apparently you can say "be still" in one billion different ways. This does not mean the message has changed, but that we are all creative in our expression of it. What resonates with one person may not with another, but what really matters is the Silence of the Teacher. In Unity the Silence of the Teacher is undeniable. This is the invitation of the universe to be still, be quite, listen, observe, and be aware and look within. It is the mind's job to think about it, complicate it and wear itself out by trying to achieve it. The good news is that in the end, despite all your effort, you are it. I can hear Buddha laughing – the laughing Buddha not the serious liberated Buddha, that is.

This is why there is no particular circumstance that will give you Unity because all is Unity and the message is the same wherever you look. The universe is constantly trying to hit you in the head; we all have just learned to keep ducking over and over again.

The fact that nobody sees this does not change the obviousness of it. In the same way, science does not understand the source of the universe yet this does not change what it actually is, even if what it is is nothing at all.

The form may change, but it all ends up the same with both dualities being seen as one. This can come about through confusion, clarity or a bump on the head. Then again you could lose it these ways too. "Gosh darn it all – I had it – then I lost it all again!"

Who had it? "I got it" Who got it? "Stop it!"

Zen Being Zen

What is Zen?

That depends on whom you ask, who is asking and who is being Zen. What is being Zen?

Zen is the art of being what is as it is. Zen is 'being' happening without an outside agent.

Is Zen Buddhist?

There is no Zen Buddhism or Zen Buddhist. If you say there is a Zen Buddhist then you have to say there is a Zen Hindu or a Zen Christian. Zen is simply being Zen.

Where do you fit into Zen?

You are Zen! You cannot get Zen because there is only Zen. Zen is what is happening with or without you. Zen is what is happening with or without time and space. Zen is 'being eternal'.

How do you reach Zen?

Zen reaches you because you are already Zen being Zen.

Being Nothingness as It is

Being nothingness is allowing what is to come and go without holding onto anything. This is the spontaneous way to be in Unity. By holding nothing you are saying "yes" to being and allowing everything to run its natural course. This is the joy and the way of nothing that defies description. The only thing that can ever stop us from seeing what is, as it is, is a concept. This may sound too simple, but ultimately it is this simple. It is too simple!

Going through the process of purification can be part of the story and indeed it usually is. Nothing is actually required, even though apparently we seem to be in a constant state of 'getting ready'. This is simply a matter of not being worthy of the total joy of being.

I am not saying don't do all of the spiritual work. On the contrary, throw yourself into it head first and explore all there is to your fullest capacity! In this way the preparation that leads to readiness can happen quicker. I am only pointing out that it is only a story that is perhaps a necessary story, as long as this 'unworthiness' or lack of readiness remains.

It makes no sense to deny this process by saying, "I am already free," since that is just another concept. No matter how much I say I am good at sports, I am still not really that sporty. Give me a chance to play volleyball for a few weeks, however, and I start to get pretty good. Even then for some reason I still have an issue with my serves. According to my Teacher, I might have something called the yips. Yips are a loss of motor control for no apparent reason. There is probably an underlying psychological issue that needs to be dealt with here. Eight out of 10 times, the ball goes to the right or left off the court. It's the yips!

So preparing by meditation, seeing your therapist, crying into or hitting a pillow, seeing a teacher, reading, taking your vitamins, chanting OM, spinning your chakras or whatever the latest thing is you are doing are all wonderful ways to prepare for 'being ready to see all there is'. Strictly speaking, however, they can be used as a distraction – to a certain extent – by the separate individual to delay being what we are.

It is rare for us to just pop completely into Unity without putting at least some effort on the spiritual path even if this effort does not look like the traditional way of seeking enlightenment. That effort might have been on attaining relative happiness, material success, a relationship or usually a combination of these plus other worldly goals.

Often dissatisfaction from not achieving what we want will lead us to seek out our true nature. Even the dissatisfaction itself can bring on a glimpse into the nothingness due to a spontaneous surrender. There have been a few sages I have respected that talk about just popping without any preparation. In these cases, they present it as something which just happened as they were walking to the beach or thinking about death or just doing something random. The separation just vanishes in their cases. Some of them say there is nothing you can do because there is no one to make it happen. They say this because, ultimately, there is no separate person. But when looking into her or his lives, often you will see a lot of preparation by 'someone'. Of course when the 'pop' happens, there is no longer any interest in what happened or any sense that 'someone' did something. Nobody did anything because there is no one, ultimately. This is the way of being nothingness as it is.

These popping events happen quite naturally, but are usually glimpses for most of us instead of ongoing stable realizations. Ironically, any previous effort made or attempted can actually be very useful in this regard. It becomes easy to stabilize being what we are when we understand what we are not. In other words, the obviousness that effortlessness is the way to go is clear when all we have done our entire life is expend effort 'to get' for example.

So it is not so much that the popping is rare, but the stabilization and integration that happens to make it permanent is rare. Your previous effort has value in this sense. You see that this effort is both useless for being nothingness and inevitable for the separate individual seeking the nothingness.

Within the story, however, there usually seems to be history of effort and seeking to various degrees depending on age and the background of the seeker. No preparation is required, yet usually something seems to happen even if it is just a curiosity about the true nature of existence.

I have seen a young girl called Priya, for example, pop into Unity. She had been seeking and meditating since around the age of 10. Before I watched the popping-ness happen I witnessed incredible focus and one-pointedness. Her dedication became absolute. No doubt there was nothing to stop her and hence she popped, since there was nothing in the way. To this day she inspires people with her focus and wisdom. They called her at the time the ancient sage in a little body.

Eventually – further down the line of experience – readiness to pop happens when we lose all hope at making ourselves happy by our little self-efforts. Hopelessness is not the usual negative giving up on life feeling. Quite the opposite – hopelessness is wonderful! Hopelessness is the relief that you cannot do it by your little self.

There is no hope! Let that sink in... Does that excite you or what? Maybe I am crazy but that means there is another possibility. The possibility is that 'you' as a separate person never did have a hope in Hell of doing it on your own. The only hope was that a miracle would happen to free you of this seeking disorder. The spontaneous readiness of being nothingness as it is is the miracle. Then the preparation can be seen as both necessary and unnecessary, depending on the perception. It is necessary as part of the story of awakening; unnecessary in being nothingness as it is.

The shining radiance of being is nothingness dancing in the story. Until this is seen we are still getting ready.

Before the Breath

Before the first breath that the body took there was only Unity. With each inhalation life is breathed into the body and then disappears into Unity. Then with the exhalation, the life breath disappears into the same Unity. A yogi or meditator can use these movements of breath to see the still point where they disappear into nothingness.

This seeing into the Stillness of the breathing process naturally happens with the practice of meditation. Upon observation it is seen that the idea that we (as separate individuals) are breathing is a false one. To see that there is no separate individual breathing is obvious. There are times when it appears the separate individual takes control of the breath to manipulate it, for example in sports such as swimming. In the spiritual breathing exercises of pranayama or if you are trying to scare someone on the phone, it can also appear that the separate individual has taken control.

When the breath is surrendered back to the source it is seen that we are literally being breathed by God or Unity itself. By watching it without manipulation, the surrendering happens automatically revealing the truth about our existence. Life is a miracle. This is a very humbling and sacred realization. Our life is quite literally in the hands of God. This applies to our heart pumping as well. If we can somehow discover this mysterious stillness at the background of the breath and heart we can follow it through the body into every one of its functions. The functioning of life is effortlessly happening everywhere – including what is closest to our perception. We begin to see its unknown influence in all activities. The stillness is before, during and after all activities of the body – yes even that one.

To say we are puppets is fitting. Our own observation will show that this puppet operates in the same way as the breath appears to move in and out of stillness. The confusion or magic trick of Maya is that the activities of the world can appear complex in their almost infinite multiplicity. We don't seem to be able to pause in daily life to see it frame by frame. But pause to see it we must!

As the breath naturally gives way into stillness, so too can all activity also be consciously given into stillness. This happens all of the time naturally, such as during sleep, although that could be considered unconscious surrendering. This is the death of the separate individual every night. Do you like the peace of a good night's sleep?

What we crave is to have this peace while the puppet is up and active. This is not only possible but also the natural way of Unity being alive and functioning in the world. Peace is the constant experience when life functions naturally without manipulation. There is an argument that all the sages who have ever just popped into Unity without a prior path did so through unconscious surrender. In other words it just happened like falling asleep. Falling 'awake' is the attempt of the spiritual seeker. To experience the profound absence of the self-identity as one does during their sleeping state and have it also appear during normal functioning while awake is perhaps the heart's highest desire.

Everything in life can be seen in the same light as what is happening before the manifestation of the breath out of the Infinite. Included are thoughts, emotions and yes even 'you' and 'me'. It is the Infinite's fault for breathing so darn much. Unity is effortlessly breathing life as it is without interference by a 'watchamacallit'.

Exploring the Self Without the Self

As familiarity with the Silence becomes 'second nature', the exploration happens as if by itself. It seems very crazy to imagine that our 'progress' will continue even without us being in charge of it. How this happens is one of the most amazing mysteries. After all, what can the self gain from 'progress' since it is already complete?

Understanding this expansion is possible if we view it from Unity's perspective. From this perspective, there has never actually been separation between oneness and multiplicity. The many is simply an appearance in the mirror of all there is. In other words the progress of moving towards infinite expansion is notional. Progress is a part of the story. I don't bring this up so that we can ignore or deny the evolution of consciousness, but to point to the obviousness that from this perspective it is easy to imagine how one could progress even if there is no separate person to make progress.

The separate person has disappeared into Unity, but to the outside world that person still appears to live and breathe and go shopping, bowling etc. In this way the mysterious exploration continues as a story of magnificent potential. It has always been a story and just continues as such. The only difference is that it is seen as it is. It continues to function 'as if' it is real even though it is a reflection in the mirror. The story is not separate from the ultimate in this sense but an expression of Love unfolding forever and beyond. It is not possible for the mind to understand, but can be intuited through insight.

After Unity, the self spontaneously realizes that Unity forever on a fresh and innocent basis. This is the essence of 'being alive' and the transformation into the miraculous-ness of living.

Again it is useful to point out that this does not mean that anything changes on the outside but rather the relationship with everything is seen in a new light. That there was never any control was already the case. That may or may not be your experience, however, but nonetheless the separate individual only has an illusion of control. This illusion comes from the belief that it is the source, the pretend-subject. It has appeared – like an image in the mirror – to be in charge of the events happening in life. It is understandable that it takes this position since any other idea seems to be a crazy and scary option from this perception.

With the discovery and play of the Silence, the underlying energy to do and evolve through life is seen in a clear light. Without holding onto this wellspring of energy, the spirit naturally moves through manifestation like a kind of director. The interesting fact is that it is really more a spontaneous directing without any separate entity to direct. This is the miracle of consciousness and could be seen as the Holy Spirit in action.

It is not that this spontaneity is new. It has always been like this even in the complete ignorance of the true nature. The images in the mirror of Unity have always been doing their image-dancing or imagining. The same divine energy has been moving through the character forever, only there has been a filter that thinks it is separate. Science has seen that there is actually a time delay for this phenomenon of claiming ownership. There is spontaneous action and then the sense 'I am doing it, I am thinking it etc' comes in a split-second after.

I understand that this is conceptual until it is seen, but it is interesting to hear it nonetheless. Within the Unity of self the act of ego, sense of self, owning, me, mine, and the fake subject as it appears to take control of the puppet is also spontaneous. Everything that follows from appearing to be separate at this point, such as anxiety, fear, superiority, inferiority and responsibility all are the spontaneous results of this simple error in perception. The error as well is also a spontaneous happening in Unity since Unity is all there is.

This concept demonstrates that the obvious truth is that,

whether or not there is recognition of your true nature, it does not change your status of being one with God and the Universe. The idea of separation is a function of what is happening and all the identifications are only a side effect of Maya, or illusion. The problem of being separate from this point of view is not really a problem but a simple misdirection of attention. The self in Unity has moved attention from its infinite status to an object that thinks it is the subject. Since this pretend subject is attached to the body then it can only think in terms of a 'you', a 'me' and 'others'. Other objects are also masquerading as subjects aka the 'people or humans' of the world.

The dance we do from this separate point of view is still the infinite dancing without actually becoming separate. This is the great distinction and Joke we are faced with... not being separate in reality, but thinking we are separate.

Both the ideas of separate individual and the 'external' God as director are seen to be conceptual. The mind simply cannot explain the miracle of the self exploring the Self without the small 's' 'self' because there is nothing to identify and grasp by the mind as 'the director'. This seems illogical and impossible because how can we have an effect without a cause? The reason is that the cause and the effect are notions in the mirror of Unity. The intellect always needs a cause, which is the cause of its limitation to see the causeless. To the intellect, this world of big 'S' Self is absolute craziness because there is no control. It is absolutely right!

This absolute craziness from the intellects' point of view is the absolute freedom of Unity.

Having Your Cake & Eating It Too

Unity is not about being above and beyond everything. This would not be complete. Unity is about having your cake and eating it too. This is the Infinite.

What does the infinite include? It includes nothing and everything.

When talking about Unity we talk about the dissolution of the separate individual. While this is true, it can of course be misinterpreted. In fact it can only be misunderstood if the intellect is involved. The fact is that this 'loss or death' in one sense is an incredible invitation to have everything – including 'all of yourself'. How can death or loss give you all of yourself?

Unity is the complete freedom to be you. What is missing is the identification with a you as 'separate'. This you still comes and goes with its personality and flavor as it always has. Your neighbor still annoys you like he always did, but you are not there to care about the annoyance as it comes and goes. Instead of taking yourself seriously, now you can pretend to take yourself seriously. Pretending is fun. When we were children we did it all the time. Now I am pretending to be a responsible grown-up. The world is simply a playground for this innocent magic.

This pretending is not irresponsible like pretending to pay your landlord by giving them an empty envelope. Pretending to be responsible is about not taking ownership of everything. In Unity this pretending is natural; not just a practice but also the way things are. This is living the old saying "being in the world but not of it".

In a very strange and paradoxical way, losing your separate ego allows you to finally be your ego character without the strings attached. Isn't it ironic that what the world tells us will make a happier ego makes a miserable ego instead? The only way for the ego to be happy is through losing itself in the Silence. This is not a tragedy since the ego has never existed as the source. It is a pretend source. The relief from the heavy burden of carrying this source on its fake shoulders is immense. The ego is not a mistake that needs to be corrected. It is a simple coincidence or accident. It is consciousness saying, "Oops," and nothing more profound than that.

It is an imposter. As long as it thinks it is in charge it is a grumpy imposter. In Unity, it is a happy pretender in service of the divine. It can act upset, frustrated or get sad, but it is all just an act. This is the divine comedy in full swing; and by approaching this 'ego' with a sense of humor, things automatically lighten up.

In Unity you don't lose the ability to be here and play. In fact now you can really play and enjoy the ego because it is seen to be a wonderful magician. Of course you don't have to wait for anything to happen before doing that since all there is is this lightness of play already.

If the intellect could understand this, it would jump at the chance to dissolve into the Silence. It is simple logic. Dissolve into nothingness to get everything-ness. Who gets to own this everything-ness? Who would need to claim it when there is no separate source?

All that actually disappears is the weight of the concept of being in control. The ego, from one perspective, is the illusion of being the source of the character of you. The character of you is a part of the play of life and does not need to be manipulated by this 'false center of operations'.

In Unity you have the illusion of being separate and being totally free from the illusion at the same time. This is the essence of being beyond duality and non-duality. This is having your cake and eating it too. In Unity cake tastes 50 times better than in separation. Why does cake taste better? Cake tastes better because there is not a separate individual eating it. A separate individual can only take in so much enjoyment. In Unity, the entire Universe is enjoying the cake because there is no separate someone eating the cake. There is no limit to the wonder of this cake and the expansion it brings. Watch out for the expansion part – if you know what I mean.

In fact, this cheesecake tastes way too good, I would just focus on eating broccoli instead.

The Source of Consciousness

Consciousness has been described in many different ways by different people. Similar to the word ego, it has many variations on its definition. The best thing we can do is forget about understanding and go with our direct experience of the Silence. Through our experience of the Silence, all wisdom spontaneously comes from the intuition of Unity. This does not mean the true definition will pop up in bright lights in your head, although that power would have been very useful for me while in school.

Keep in mind that all descriptions are conceptual. On a higher level everything is literally conceptual, including this and this and yes even that is also conceptual. Feel free to point at whatever objects are nearby to match the preceding sentence.

Unity is listening without conceptualizing. Concepts are useful in the spiritual game if they point to Silence or give an opportunity to the intellect to 'get it'. What is important about understanding? Understanding is only important to relax the intellect. In this way, the readiness to pop unfolds.

The concepts of pure awareness, pure consciousness and even Silence are given as pointers. The experiencing of these is a whole other ballgame and does not require understanding. In fact, my favorite of all the enlightened ones is the blissful idiot who is simply 'free'. He does not care about these fancy words, but only loves to be all there is. What else could he be interested in?

Do not be afraid of 'I Don't Know!' Embrace I don't know because that is all you need to know, you know!

Consciousness is all there is. It has no source except if you want to call nothingness its source; but there is no difference between the two.

Finding the Way Home through the Maze

People and mice from all over the world love to go to labyrinths and mazes. It is an ancient tradition in many cultures. Some do it as a sacred spiritual act or because some divine being – or scientist in the case of mice – put them there, while others do it just for fun. Fun is the correct attitude to approach the maze and this subject of Unity. If you treat the world and your place in it as a kind of puzzle or maze it turns the quest for Unity into a fun game. Can you find your way out?

What if there was a maze so tricky that you could not tell that you were already out of it? What if it is way too obvious for you to get it? Wouldn't that be funny and possibly even ironic?

Now that is a super maze! As you are trying to find your way to enlightenment through the maze, do not underestimate the power of trickery going on, otherwise called Maya or Samsara. This is why it is almost impossible for people to find their way out without some kind of guide who has walked through it before.

In this maze you will find people selling maps that say, "Here's how to get out of the maze, the quickest!" This book is one of them. Don't trust these vendors – including me – blindly! All you have to do is follow their maps for a while and see you are getting nowhere. This is the invitation to go inward and hopefully those you trust and see as wise point you in that direction.

After being lost and frustrated for awhile we will be attracted to another vendor in the maze. "Okay," we say, "I have tried thousands of these maps and still I can't find my way out, what map or a-maze-zing GPS system are you selling?"

"I am not a vendor," says the grizzled old vendor. "I have nothing to sell you because all the maps are useless. Obviously you are looking for a way out and I can help you with this if you are willing to do what I ask." We say, "We have wandered this maze for millennia and have found nothing but more twists and turns, of course we will do anything, we have lost all hope that a map will get us there!"

Wizened old vendor, with a gleam in his eye, "First of all, listen to what is behind the words I am speaking. Listen with your heart, not your head. Please do this and you will be fine. All I want for you is for you to see that you are already free. I myself had been wandering here a long time, but recently I came across a vendor who, like myself, also had no maps to sell me but only pointed to the way. The vendor helped me to see that I could not find my way out on my own. Believe me when I say I have tried more than most I see wandering through here. I had been told that my intelligence is of the greatest in this world and my devotion to escaping is the purest, yet still I could not escape even with the most advanced tools."

The old codger goes on, "Nothing I am going to tell you is new. I can only convey to the best of my ability what this vendor shared with me. Understand that what was shared had nothing to do with the maps we have been so focused on all this time. This new sharing was off the map and cannot be shared in the same way we are used to. The bottom line is that we have been going about it the hard way by taking the maps and even the vendors seriously. What I'm telling you might come as a shock and even sound ridiculous, but I assure you it is my own direct experience. You are not lost in a maze, nor are you in a maze at all. The maze is merely but that you think you are lost. In truth, you have always been free, even while you seemed to be lost here. I did not believe this when it was told to me either, but after seeing the evidence I could no longer deny it and I stopped selling the maps altogether. I threw them all into the fire – so to speak – because of my devotion and inability to get anywhere."

I know what you are thinking... HOW! You are screaming how! Become intimate with the Silence. The obvious will become clear.

Throwing Away the Ladder

By continuing to rely on outside information for advancement, including wise information, we avoid or delay the joy of discovering what is real about this instant.

Having a ladder of knowledge can serve us as long as something tangible can be reached at the top. In terms of Unity, this is impossible and can only be a hindrance to actual revelation or delighting in the awareness of reality. That is not to say that the ladder is not a necessary part of the story. It seems logical that to reach a conceptual liberation you would need a conceptual ladder. This is conceptually very true.

The whole point of the conceptual spiritual quest is to get to the top and have a look around. Once you get there, then what?

At this moment it becomes clear that you have been merely climbing inside your head. You have been traveling from ignorance, and as you got higher and higher you were gaining greater conceptual freedom. Maybe we understand that, but what happens when you get to the top?

This is the point when we would think whatever idea we have of enlightenment would be fulfilled. From one point of view, the path looks like climbing a ladder to get to the top. From another, it is simply seeing what is real about this moment. If we throw away the ladder, no matter how uncomfortable that might be, we open up to a greater view of what is happening right now. This gives us the opportunity to see the obvious.

Perhaps this throwing away is simply shaking our head after realizing we were imagining the whole trip up and down, getting closer and then falling off again. This shaky position seems so high we could fall, so we keep looking for bigger, sturdier ladders and then move onto a new mental scaffolding.

The fear of the unknown can be strong if we have been relying upon our familiar system of beliefs to get us to where we think we are going. If we are honest, however, we can see that many if not all of them won't serve our highest desires. This is so because that which is real we already have and it needs no external device to support it. It is this support and grounding of the Silence that we are already standing in. Heaven – referring to the heaven of Unity – isn't 50,000 feet above; it is here and even far below. In fact, there is nowhere that it is not. Anything that is useful for going inward into the unknown is only a tool that can be forgotten once we've arrived.

Even the greatest of meditation tools or any other tool designed to bring us inward is surrendered ultimately. Take for example the breath, which is surrendered each time we breathe, and yet it is one of the most ancient and useful practices for going inward. It is used in yoga and meditation classes around the world today, as it has been for millennia. Yet even if we cling to something as simple as the breath it trivializes the reality behind it making it seem superficial. We can manipulate it or we can simply see the natural movement, which is automatically moving inward and taking the breath and therefore our attention to the source.

The mind thinks in terms of progress and climbing a ladder. It has evidence in the world to convince it that indeed this is what is required. If I keep climbing, eventually I will get to the top. For the separate individual climber a ladder is a part of the deal, but how can you climb when you are already standing in what you are? Is there really a ladder? Or is it a product of imagination? Did somebody tell you need it? Did you read about it somewhere? Were you watching Oprah again? Don't get me wrong, who doesn't like Oprah? I Love Oprah! Oh stop it; I am going to start crying now.

The conceptual ladder is only superficial in the end. If it is real to you, then the best thing you can do is keep going higher and don't look down. The faster you fall off the quicker you can see the ground of being where you already are!

Being Without What?

Often when we are referring to surrender or letting go there is the sense of loss. We are losing or being asked to give up things on this spiritual path of surrender. Usually this can seem nice, especially when we talk about losing attachments, addictions, fears etc. Sounds lovely doesn't it? "Of course I want to lose my paranoia, anxiety and fear of chipmunks!"

By surrendering, what are we really losing and what is it like to be without it? How can we really know if it is not our own direct experience?

It is threatening to our need of survival to think of 'losing our self in the Silence' or 'dissolving into the unknown'. This makes sense since it is very natural to want to survive. We can't blame the ego for desiring to live, who would sanely want death anyway? There is a misconception about this whole notion, however, especially in relationship to being without an ego, aka 'enlightenment'.

Unfortunately this again can only be conceptual unless it is actually what is being lived in Unity. It can be glimpsed, but even then there is still a fear of what might be perceived as total annihilation or extinction. That sounds scary to me too. Yikes!

We will never know because as long as perception is from a limited point of view, it cannot help but be in the way of seeing the completeness of the absence of 'me'. That being said, the disappearance of the ego does happen spontaneously all of the time without being a big deal at all. We hardly notice the thousands of times it disappears like it is the blinking of an eye. This hints at the ease of the experience that awaits when we get 'our' enlightenment.

When it is understood in this way it becomes very obvious that the fear is irrational, but then again we have no control over it anyway. In Unity, loss and gain are both conceptual, as are the notions of life and death, born and unborn. All duality is only conceptual, from the Unity perspective. Upon waking up, which is the death of the ego, the loss is apparent only because the ego is forever a phantom. Until the actual moment of its permanent disappearance or the seeing that all there is is 'THIS', fear is an understandably common and a sane response. In some but not all cases prior to seeing reality there can be a pulling back out of fear.

At this point we can say that there is nothing to worry about and seeking the company of sages or someone who can understand this type of 'death' could be useful. All we can do is jump. Has someone ever pushed you into the water when you were not looking?

When I was around 5 I had a not too serious skiing accident and had to be picked up by the ski patrol. A few years later when we went on a school ski trip, I was on the top of a mountain looking down and was terrified because of that memory. I had decided to walk down to avoid skiing down the run and just then two school bullies came up to me and said, "Have fun," as they pushed me down the hill. I screamed, "NO!" and went straight down at super speed. I could not stop because I did not even know the snowplow technique. It was indeed fun, even when I lost control and became a huge snowball of joy.

Once you get pushed off, no matter how you were pushed – nicely or by two evil boys – you are going! This can be the cosmic Oomph that pushes you off the cliff. Then oops it's done.

Just One More Thing

Be forewarned that in the story there are always more things that
need to happen before we will surrender into what is real permanently. There is always 'one more thing' to let go of. One more
profound experience, one more teaching, one more book, one
more teacher, one more concept, one more shot of tequila and one
more chakra to activate. The list is never ending.

Do not underestimate the power of the mind to keep adding
to the list. It will keep going until you die. In fact you will never
be ready if you are listening to the mind. This is where surrender
into the unknown no matter how it seems is the only way to go.
The sense of needing to experience 'one more thing' was a strong
addiction that seemed to keep me locked into the next thing that
would bring me closer to freedom.

Underlying this process was a deep unworthiness which was
motivating the need to keep purifying and preparing. Despite
being at least intellectually aware that this is only a fantasy, it was
still very real to me and seemed to always keep what I wanted
most at a distance. Even though it was pointed out that more
experiences were not necessary, I still could not break this
pattern.

The bottom line is experiences don't lead to Unity, yet happen
within it or on it as reflection on a mirror. Experiences are a part
of the story and are real for the separate individual that apparently experiences them. Of course this seeming 'way to live' is
unavoidable and can only be seen as part of the process of getting
ready for freedom, love or whatever happens to be the highest
desire.

It can be seen that 'getting ready' is futile and by adding one
more thing we are only delaying the reality of this instant. Unity
has nothing to do with worthiness, and an honest exploration of
the Silence reveals that purification is only a belief of the separate

individual. Until the obviousness of Unity is seen, however, we are indeed helpless and just keep purifying. Grabbing onto a concept that 'I am pure already' is just 'one more thing' to let go of.

Ultimately, surrendering to the unknown is the only thing that makes sense and the separate self's continued insistence on 'needing to' gets dissolved into the love of all there is. This love has no worth and no need since it is already complete in its limitlessness.

Stealing from the Absolute

It is not an overstatement to say that everyone is taking from the Silence what is not his or hers. Yes, we are stealing. I know your mother said, "Do not steal," and there you go anyway. Okay I will let you get away with the stuff you are not conscious of, but concerning the conscious stuff, shame on you.

All thoughts, feelings and actions come from and return to the Silence. That is, they return unless you grab them and identify with them as mine. This is what the separate individual does; it steals from what is not for it to claim as exclusively mine. Thank God the Silence does not care and forgives us instantly while it patiently awaits the return of all its goodies. The scary thing is that it even allows the stealing of 'being the source'. This is all the ego is – an egocentric idea of 'being the source'. What is the essence of this? It is a concept of being the source of thoughts, feelings and actions. It continues to do this even with the overwhelming evidence to the contrary, which you will know through your own practice of self-inquiry and meditation.

You can be fully aware of this silly idea and yet there you go continuing to be separate. This is the game of waking up, is it not? It is kind of crazy, but it does not have to be too difficult once the separate individual is seen for what it is... merely a concept. Not 'you' in your divine nature, but the idea of 'you' as separate and apart.

This is not pseudo-science. This is matter-of-fact kindergarten stuff and is easily seen while observing what happens in the average mind. Probably better to stick with your mind first before fishing around someone else's. You might find some of your thoughts floating around out there in the minds of others as well.

The pseudo-subject or separate subject thinks that it is the center of the personal universe. Therefore it feels entitled to own what comes and goes. Then this subject will have the weight of taking responsibility for everything that it takes and does. This is why sometimes we feel so heavy like the world is on our shoulders. No wonder we feel so guilty for no reason, like we did something wrong. This can be a root stress.

This type of stealing is like my neighbor Bob taking my lawnmower because it looks exactly the same. Have you seen people at a party walk away with someone else's shoes or coat because they look similar? Or more common are those that walk away with someone else's drink. It is not their fault; it's a simple mistake. The pseudo subject is a thief in disguise. This thief is terrified of being found out, and for good reason. It is a mouse dressed up as a cat in a room full of hungry big cats... meow.

When this thief is caught, it vanishes into the absolute. Seeing that it comes and goes like what it steals is a wonderful start.

Ignorance

Ignorance does not exist in Unity. Since all there is is Unity, ignorance does not exist period. Ignorance is only a mirage or apparent dream in a story that runs simultaneous to reality. It is the classic image in the mirror that gives it its substance. It is designed in such a way as to make the mistake of deception an easy one to make. Like looking in the mirror and seeing 'you'. No matter how much you think or believe it is you that is being looked at, it is not true. Not only is it not you as a personality, it is literally not you as a body with a face. It is only an appearance of an appearance within Unity.

This does not change the fact that 99.99% of the people of the world see these deceptive images as you, another, or me. The mirror makes it incredibly easy to fall into this identification. It is not the mirror's fault that it reflects so well. In the same way, it is not the fault of truth that there seems to be ignorance. The root of ignorance is to ignore. What is being ignored? What is being ignored right now?

The average Joanne (no offence intended or implied to any actual apparent persons named Joanne) lives in a state of total distraction and avoidance of what is already obvious. This has happened to the point that seeing this obviousness is a rarity. A little inspiration and understanding can go a long way to open up to all there is. Once that fire is kindled in the heart, the seeing cannot be that far away. Once the glimpse into Unity happens, the game is over.

So why are we in such a mess?

It is only a conceptual mess brought about through crazy thinking. The separate individual is a mirage and we say it is in ignorance of reality. How is a mirage capable of being ignorant? Does the mirage wake up and see its own mirage-ness? Does the image in the mirror suddenly wake up and see that it is only an appearance?

Not seeing truth is only a simple misdirection of attention; a sleight of hand like illusionists use. The act of not seeing does not make a mirage real no matter how long we believe in it. Staring at the image in the mirror is fascinating and we can make it do anything we want; but whenever we take attention away from it, it ceases to be.

Character Building

One of the misleading assumptions is that once we wake up we never have to deal with our character. It may be true that it is not the essence of what we are. It may be true that we see through the appearance of it into the Silence, which seems to breathe life into it. That all may be true, but the idea that the disappearance of the ego or separate individual will somehow turn us into a perfect human (some humans are more perfect than others wink-wink) is simply not true. The character continues to be an expression of all there is as it always has been. Now that it is free of all the weight of personal identification, it can shine.

The idea that Unity builds character can be seen if you look at the big picture. The character is an appearance happening on the mirror, and it seems to have developed out of nothing, just like the story. The mind likes to think in terms of cause and effect. Since there is only Unity, however, to say that Unity is the cause of the character is not exactly true. Yet the character, along with the story, continues to evolve or devolve as the case may be.

So the process of character building happens in Unity both 'before', during and 'after' liberation. From the split mind Unity – also often referred to as God or Source – seems to be the cause of the character. After Unity, the character is seen in Oneness with all there is. It is no different from a flower or a tractor; and in truth, Unity becomes more like a 'tractor' beam for it.

All great sages, along with their story and character, go through periods of settling into this Oneness. We only hear about a few that have become famous and because of their fame we tend to mold our ideas around those stories. Often we judge the book by the cover. We don't bother to read the whole book about the sage because we are only interested in the 'good stuff', which usually means the last chapter. We don't see the entire story surrounding the sage, and instead see the end results and then compare our current state with theirs. What we see when we look behind the scenes of this sage – whether literally or intuitively – is a tapestry that has spontaneously shaped the image that we see. More often than not this did not happen overnight, but is an ongoing refinement of the image that is presented in the world. Indeed the highest truth is that we are all just business cards for Unity.

Even the full realization of Unity does not erase all of the conditioning and programming associated with our character or puppet. What it erases is the false identification with the separate character. In fact, nobody may even notice a single difference about this character at all! This is terrible news for the wannabe-enlightened ego. It says, "What will make me stand out from the crowd if that is the case? What will make me special?"

This is the danger of having a glimpse of Unity because the ego may claim it and say, "I got it!" then it throws on a robe, picks up a microphone and starts teaching or preaching. All that happened was a glimpse of All There Is. The ironic thing is that during the glimpse the ego was not even there and yet this resurrected super-ego may spend an entire lifetime erroneously teaching people how to wake up. I won't mention any names, but you know who you are.

Maybe you will be recognized or maybe not, but that is not up to you. Your character will get what it needs to grow up and mature into a fully functioning sage capable of great things. These great things might look like teaching thousands a mantra like "goo goo" or it may mean making blueberry pancakes for your girlfriend/boyfriend. The world does not disappear when we wake up. We may make it disappear by heading into retreats to gather momentum on a path of joy. This can be an important chapter in the book, but it is only the beginning. Ultimately what happens to our character (aka Unity's business card) is a mystery since the puppet no longer has any more strings. Will we keep the card in our pocket, will we hand it out or will we try to get it a shiny new image. After Unity all of this is only a matter of fun and play. We play with what God gave us. We got Unity and a business card, that is it.

In Unity there is no more separation or control. To try to control and run the life of the character would not only be silly but it only results in incredible pain at this point. The character sometimes ends up in places it would rather avoid. This is wonderful because it has no choice anymore. It gets what it needs to shine. It has preferences yes, but the final say is up to God. The cosmic oomph will push you into places that may be uncomfortable, to give the character a shiny new perspective or maybe to give it more humility. It would be much easier to sit on a pink cloud, but would you really want to do that? I would do it if it were cotton candy because then I could eat it.

Maybe it wants to stay in the cave to avoid the further expansion that comes from being in the 'marketplace' with those normal people. Sometimes we keep the card in the wallet or purse because there is still a fear of coming out of the Unity closet. There is nothing to fear. I am not suggesting that you run around telling people 'I' am free, look at me! No! What I am suggesting is that Unity is sharing all there is and all there is includes your shiny expression, whatever that looks like. In other words just being 'you' happens. The character still has characteristics; this is common sense. Unity is not separate from what is happening with this character, even if it does not match what we think it should look like.

Very quickly we see that resistance does not work before or after freedom. All we can do is keep walking straight ahead on the razor's edge. Through waking up we gain deep insight into what it means to be human. It is the beginning of character building without having to focus on the separate individual improving. It is an impersonal adventure of continually letting go and seeing everything coming from the Silence for what it is. There is no need to hold anything back anymore. Subtle ideas, beliefs and concepts can present themselves to be seen as long as we are exploring the infinite. As a result of this seeing, the ability to stand fully open and free as a human becomes more stable. It is because of this that we can be in the world, but not of it.

There is always more to see, hence the word and concept of infinity. The difference is that the further along a path of joy one finds oneself, the less 'personal' resistance is. It becomes a natural seeing into and through the character. It is an exciting adventure because it is not about us getting something for the little 'me' anymore. It is 'exploring the self without the self' just for the fun of it.

It may seem like a paradox or even the opposite of freedom that you can work on yourself. The truth is it is an incredibly alive and liberating experience to 'work' on your self without any reason or agenda. It is simply a function of the story and in the story there is a character. Of course if you are content doing nothing then that is fine as well.

Despite what we have been taught, the character is not a static thing. The idea that after achieving freedom you just sit around, smile and drool all day is not really that ideal if you have kids to feed, a dog to walk or even just a job to attend to as part of participating in greater society.

After Unity it is seen that no longer is life about 'you' but rather 'what you can give'. What do you have to give? A smile? A hug? Then smile and hug like a maniac.

All we have are these puppets and that which is shining through them. The universe is teaching them how to dance, often in the most unlikely of ways. Surprise!

Unity & the Energetic System

There are many schools of thought around what an energy system is. There are the chakras of the Ayurvedic system, there is the body meridian system of TCM, or Traditional Chinese Medicine, and of course there is the plain old nervous system. Whichever way we conceptualize it, this energy system responds directly to our relationship with the Silence.

The energy system, when analyzed or even experienced, may seem complex and unmanageable. It is reasonable to see it as uncontrollable, but as we explore what happens we can simplify it for both our minds and our experience of energy as it moves throughout the body. Specifically, the more we dissolve into the Silence, the greater the capacity to experience energetically what is happening. We get in touch with subtler aspects of this system. This could often be the reason why people fear going inward. There is an intuitive sense that they will be opening up a can of energetic worms. Once familiarity with the Silence happens, the capacity allows for a greater and greater sense of ease relating to the energy flowing within this system.

Before what was labeled as 'anxiety' and 'intensity' can now be seen with a new clarity. This is one of the greatest mysteries and a whole book could be written just on the subject of energy and emotion. What are energy and emotion? Or is energy in motion in relationship to the Silence and the nervous system a more apt description?

Simply put, all there is is Unity. The Silence and Unity are one and the same. Within the Silence is an energetic system that receives pure energy from the stillness. This is called the Wu in Taoist terms. The Wu is the nothingness from which anything and any energy can happen. Everyone wants the Wu whether they know it or not. It is the fundamental goal behind all activities – aside from meditation – such as physical sports, yoga, chi-gong and tai chi etc. There is no difference between Wu and Silence.

Every human has a nervous/energetic system that is uniquely experiencing and translating this Wu right now. The pure energy or Wu hits this system and is translated or perceived as thousands of possible forms from subtle to intense. As this energy gets received, the brain gets activated and translates it. On the surface this can take any number of forms from thinking to feeling to experiencing plain old nothing at all.

The motivation behind all therapies, modalities and the spiritual quest itself is to be able to change, heal or calm the energy. From the ego perspective, it is to get rid of what is perceived as the negative energy. There is nothing wrong with wanting the pure energy of Wu in the body. In fact it feels wonderful and is a healthy thing for the nervous system and sign of a balanced mind/body.

On our individual paths we may have learned how to manipulate these energies positively or negatively through intention. One thing for certain is that on a spiritual path we have a tendency to only want 'good vibes' and 'good energy'. We have learned to treat this as a sign of progress or how close we are to achieving Unity. We check in and then based on this energy in the body determine if we are doing 'well' or not according to our idea or ideal vision of 'peace'.

The separate subject thinks in terms of peace and pain when it looks into its energetic system. It is not a whole view obviously, because it is separate; therefore it must see it in duality. What it does not know is that it is already in the peace of Wu and all there is. The duality of little 'p' peace and pain are only fluctuations within Wu perceived – very superficially – by this separate subject in the energy system. As long as we identify with ourselves as separate, we will claim ownership of this energetic system to various degrees. This is normal and our relationship with what is happening internally will change as our experience with the Silence and therefore Wu becomes more intimate.

It is always possible to change energy by manipulation. For example by eating healthy food, exercising, doing chi-gong, yoga, meditating, taking Chinese herbs and being in the company of the wise, chances are that the energy system will start to smooth out. Yet even if we are doing these things on an island paradise of our choosing, this still does not guarantee that there will not be some kind of intense activity there. As long as the separate subject is doing the viewing we have no choice but to see it as separate. This means you can relax and just be yourself! When it gets rough, just take a deep breath into your stomach and try to laugh about it.

In fact to the horror of many who go to meditation retreats (or on a vacation paradise) they find that they are confronted with huge amounts of stress. If the retreat is designed to explore the Silence, there will be no focus on the stress or drama itself; however, the stress coming up is a part of the clearing of the energetic system. The 'stuff' comes up only to be released from the system. So instead of a vacation to get away, stress is released which is actually much more valuable than any superficial trip to your idea of a paradise. Both together are preferable of course.

This unloading of the nervous system does not require manipulation; and in fact, any attempt to change what is happening can hold back the full aliveness of what is. This is in a sense allowing love to finally burst through the system. Anything that may be in the way can and does come up. This can be expected. Release does not necessarily mean a drama, however, and there is no need to look back or analyze a single thing. Talking about it can be useful as long as the person who you speak with does not default to seeing you as broken.

Healing of this system is natural as we explore what does not change. If allowed, it can be embraced with gentleness and compassion. We are learning how to not take things seriously, after all. When we have taken something seriously, like a traumatic event, we can also expect it to be hard to take it lightly. With practice, allowing of the release becomes easier. We begin to accept what is happening energetically, which includes the stories, emotions and the sense of separation. With a glimpse of Unity, there is no one to disagree with what is happening. This is the Silence being 'okay' with what is.

In Unity the relationship with the nervous system becomes like an open field. This does not imply that nothing happens in the field, however. There can be tremendous activity as we become more in tune with movements, sensations and energies.

This is aliveness.

Psychology & Unity

Notice the chapter is not called "The Psychology of Unity" because there is no such thing. I am not writing as a psychologist here, but as a patient of psychology – aren't we all – explorer of the psyche or peeler of the onion, if you will.

Our psychological makeup, personality and mind as well as any conceptual breakdown of these terms happen within Unity. In my personal experience, when we start to entertain ideas wrapped around the ego and psychology, we can open up a world of confusion and the stubborn notion of 'holding onto what we know'. Again this is why I like the term 'nothing' to describe everything. This keeps it simple plus it is actually more accurate; at least in the realm of perception it is the clearest term I have found. The spiritual quest can become confusing when starting to mistake a healthy psychology for being free. They seem to be the same thing. They are not!

Falling apart can actually be healthier than having it together. Remember, I started this book by saying that I'll be working backwards to the usual forward thinking. This makes sense since we are falling back into our selves or falling awake. I am not saying that psychological health is not useful or even necessary to live a happy life. Unity, however, does not care about the state of the mind or psychology. The Silence is already all there is and the spiritual quest is about discovering the unchanging-ness of that. It is equally there for the sane or the insane. This is love in the most beautiful way we can imagine. Unconditional love does not care about states of consciousness or unconsciousness.

So what do we do with our insanity? Let it continue to be there, but play in the discovery of getting sane. Explore the Zen of how! Find out ways in which you can be healthier and happier. If you make discovering the Silence important then the psychology of your 'you' will have a greater chance to heal. Of course I can't give a general rule since there are many degrees and apparent levels of insanity. Simply put, regardless of the levels, we are all insane to one degree or another. Simply observing ourselves and others will show this to be the case.

As we build up our 'characters' and work on our 'issues' this can be a tremendous benefit to letting go of the past and adds to our overall well-being. Working on our psycho-self in this way can be a preparation for the willingness to dive into a path of joy.

By being on a path of joy and giving attention to what does not change we see through the psycho-self bit by bit. It is not that we need to change its structure and so-called 'faults', but we simply see it. As a result we care less and less about its crazy operations.

That being said, I have personally seen that there are healings and insights into the psychology that could be called miraculous. The healing is miraculous in that no effort was needed on the part of the separate individual. For example, we have been working on forgiving mother or father for years and now all of a sudden we notice that it is no longer an issue of interest. The forgiveness has happened without us lifting a finger or doing any 'work' at all.

As we approach the Silence and therefore Unity, the psycho-self gets bathed in pure consciousness. As this happens, the obvious pops up and the weight of being attached to the psychology of our small 's' self loosens. We don't lose our grip on reality as many may fear – the sense of falling apart or 'losing it' is very common at some point with prolonged meditation – instead we lose our grip on the ownership of the psychology. We see that the psychology of our 'self' is merely happening. That being said, there can be a genuine 'I am falling apart' sensation, at least that was my experience. Just fall awake!

No matter how healthy or unhealthy the state of mental health may appear, try to remember it is still an appearance within Unity. We are all crazy and can allow ourselves the space to love and accept this craziness. This acceptance gives us the space to understand what is happening through working on ourselves – in whatever way that presents – while continuing to walk a path of joy. This also gives us more of the capacity to love and be compassionate to others going through their craziness themselves. We are not alone.

I have met wonderful teachers of meditation who have been labeled with 'mental disorders', such as bipolar disorder or schizophrenia. This does not limit them at all. They take their medication as prescribed because of the 'imbalance' in the brain and keep going. In fact, can you imagine the joy and inspiration as someone is faced with serious mental illness finds him or her. Suddenly it becomes very clear that the 'disorder' is not personal, now they can share with them their direct experience of what it is like to live with the psycho-self and live in peace and contentment at the same time.

I remember a student on a retreat who was suffering with anxiety. As he was sharing what it was like, it felt as if I was in his body and living the exact thing. I knew energetically exactly the sensations happening at the time. The only apparent difference was that I could see through them because of the practice of exploring the Silence.

A Course in Miracles calls the teacher who has not healed himself the unhealed healer. These people are very common in the world. I have met many experts who were unhealed healers. I used to be shocked by that, but now I see it as just another fact of life. There is nothing wrong with being unhealed and having issues; after all, who doesn't have something to work on? Some of the most conscious people I have met still have psychological issues. This is part of the overall package of being human.

Becoming free is not about analyzing and dissecting the ego, it is about accepting it. Unity is not about dissolving the personality, but the identification with it. The ego, personality, and character are products of conditioning and programming and have nothing to do with Unity. They are a unique part of the story that needs love and acceptance. This psychological character does not wake up, you do. What you appear to be as the separate psychological entity – or 'psycho-self' – is seen through Unity. This is very disappointing news for anyone who has invested time and energy working on themselves, if they think that it will make them free. It is useful for the character, but does not equal Unity. Of course it doesn't hurt to have a more balanced individual in the world, much better than those sometimes annoying imbalanced ones.

The term self-actualization does not equal Unity. It means that one has accepted their character and ego as a unique human being with all that entails. So what if we become self-actualized… then what? What is the difference when we still die as a happy ego in separation?

The nice thing about Unity or glimpses of Unity is that it is in the realm of miracles. So in the "holy instant" or "atonement" (ACIM terms) some psychological issues and/or trauma that one is faced with can be completely dissolved leaving no trace. That can be a lovely bonus of the Unity glimpse, but there are no guarantees. Staying open to see our issues is the key; when we see them, we keep letting them go. Discovering what the Silence is with clarity is the way to an effortless process of letting go.

While it is true freedom can happen without ever looking at forgiving your mother or letting go of anger for your father, I think it is always useful to not avoid these things. By staying open to heal, the openness itself will bring whatever healing we need. It could look like seeing a counselor; a shamanic journey or maybe it just vanishes into the 'nowhere' where it came from.

The Silence can be used as an escape method rather than as a natural way to be. There is nothing to fear about the screwed-up-ness of our psycho-self. When the one-pointedness of dissolving in the Silence is combined with gentle allowing and acceptance of the small 's' self, the end result can only be a miracle. We could rename this new self the "psychologically balanced unified non-separate self" or call it "self-actualized Unity" but whatever it is, it is certainly a lot of unconditional love.

Cosmic Oomph

From the perspective of separation, it is very difficult to understand that by letting go into the Silence what we want will happen for us. How can we be sure without being in control? We can't! This is the fear of not knowing.

When we are not in control, there are no more guarantees. How can I even wake up if I don't keep pushing myself forward? There is a natural energy that can be called the 'cosmic oomph'. This energy is like a gentle push that spontaneously moves consciousness to its highest potential. It does not need a separate pusher.

The natural inclination of the Infinite is to explore what it is. This happens out of the love and passion for all there is. The oomph is the 'zip' or 'zing' that gives the exact amount of divine energy needed for the expansion of dissolution to happen. It is completely mysterious and indescribable. There is no way to predict it. Suddenly there it is and before you know what has happened, you are in the fresh aliveness of this infinite Silence. Perhaps this is the holy spirit of love or the movement of bliss. This God-juice is way more powerful than Red Bull – and it is free too.

In Unity this cosmic oomph becomes the motivation for the dance of the puppet or character. Without an individual doer, the question remains: how am I going to live or move in the world? A seeker can get stuck in this state for a long time. It is like being in between doing and not doing, acting and not acting. This is the traditional stale state of 'nothing is happening or moving'. For the mind, this is a stuck state of being frozen in between the spirit world and the human world. This mind knows that it has no control and yet waits for something to happen. Often this can lead to depression, as life seems a boring sequence of meaningless events. This is a dry state. Not everyone, however, needs to go through this but it is still common.

From what I have seen, this state tends to drag on without the guidance of a Teacher or at least the company of the wise. In this state the ego has fallen away to a degree yet the total recognition of Unity remains hidden. The secret is not to take anything seriously. Often the student will say things like, "What is the point of life? Why bother doing anything?" If you see someone like this, just tickle her or him and say, "Jesus, lighten up, I thought all this enlightenment stuff was supposed to make you happy."

At this point the awareness of the Silence should be stable enough to keep letting go of these depressing concepts as they arise. Unfortunately I cannot give an exact time frame on when the cosmic oomph will sweep through and push 'you' off the edge of this seriousness permanently, but you can't go wrong by 'not thinking so much'!

The cosmic oomph loves life for no reason other than all there is is life. The cosmic oomph moves into 'higher awareness' for no reason other than enjoyment. The cosmic oomph is pure energy with nothing added. It POPS; and when you have no energy to enjoy life, it will step in and enjoy it on your behalf! Just keep allowing and take nothing seriously, especially your head, if you think you have one.

Obviousness

I understand that everyone who reads this will be reading from a different perception or 'level' of consciousness. I personally dislike using that "level" word, since in reality there are only appearances of levels. How these messages are perceived and received are out of my control. If in some way the clarity comes that "everything is actually a lot easier than I thought", then that is wonderful!

Confusion is probably the most likely response as long as we are identified with the separate individual. My Teacher once said, "Confusion is the last defense of the ego; if nothing else is working it will throw up confusion." This is wonderful as well! Confusion is the precursor to easiness as long as we keep skipping down a path of joy and don't take the confusion seriously.

In a way this cloud that gets thrown up over the obviousness of Unity is expected if it is understood that Unity cannot be comprehended with the complexity of thinking. In other words the mind needs to be dumfounded, stunned and stupefied! My Teacher also says that, "It always gets easier and if you think it's easy now – just wait." This is the obviousness of reality and the path to it. It gets easier and easier since it is clear, simple and obvious.

If it does not seem simple at this point, that is because I have complicated it and have not done justice to demonstrate to you this simplicity. That is not reality's fault, but the fault of the inter-preter or messenger. The truth is it is very difficult to describe the indescribable obviousness of all there is. This is most easily expressed by resting in Silence or nothingness whereby it can reveal itself without a messenger having to point to it. Sharing the Silence gives the clearest description of what it is because the separate individual is out of the way and the Silence is describing itself. The words do not matter when sharing the Silence because the resonance is obvious. A true Teaching or a 'path of joy' will always have this sharing as the foundation since it is the quickest way to see through the facade to the underlying Unity.

The sense that there is something you need or are missing is only a temporary perception. The universe will show you what you need as you are walking the razor's edge. The reason you don't see it is not because it is hidden or complicated, but because it is too simple and obvious.

To discover that we are already free is the most enjoyable and blissful adventure. It is the Best!

A Path of Joy

As my Teacher says, "This is a path of joy." Often he tells the story of when he was sitting with his teacher and a group of students at a retreat. His Teacher said to them, "How many of you are willing to walk through hell to get to freedom?" Like warriors they shouted out in unison, "YES!" raising their hands while growling and showing their fearless commitment on their faces.

Then he asked, "How many of you are willing to walk through joy?" They all looked at each other with confused looks, most hesitating like it was a trick question. Some waiting to see how many other hands went up before putting his or her own up. Some with the hand halfway up. Then a few brave souls put up their hands.

I love this story. Many of us would and have been willing to do almost anything to wake up. There is nothing more valuable. This is the invitation to do it, not only the quickest and most direct way, but the most joyful. In truth this is the only way to walk into Unity.

So I ask you in all sincerity and Love,

Are you willing to walk through Joy?

Glossary

Silence:
Stillness, Infinite, Eternal, Being, Self, Everything-ness, Peace, Nothingness, Freedom (feel free use your own words).
Silence and Unity are ONE.

Unconscious glimpse of Unity:
A 'glimpse' is a happening whereby the separate individual dissolves or loses itself in the Silence. The unconscious glimpse happens without a clear awareness of 'what is happening'. Suddenly the glimpse is there. Unity may continue to unfold and become more obvious, or the glimpse may seem to disappear when the separate individual returns.

Uni-intuition:
Uni-intuition is an intuitive sense of Unity or of already being free. This vision can happen with or without being consciously aware of it. This is a seeing or knowingness of being Divine, interconnected and/or one with everything. Being in nature is the prime example of this intuition but it can be enlivened anywhere.

Conscious glimpse of Unity:
Clearly seeing that there is only Silence without separation. The separate individual disappears for an apparent duration in time, seconds, minutes, hours, months, years etc. Then the separation returns. This can be a spontaneous single event or recurring.

Perception of Unity:
Unity as it is is an unchanging oneness. The Perception of Unity is ongoing and changes depending on the stability of Unity. During the process of the stabilization of Unity, the perception refines and clarity increases. After Unity, the clarity of perception

continues to refine and to reveal the Infinity of Unity. Perception after Unity becomes more accurately described as "seeing with the Unity goggles". This way of seeing allows for the light of consciousness to expand.

Unity:
A stabilized ongoing Silence experiencing everything as it is without separation. It is indescribable.

This:
What is happening now. All there is.

Separate individual:
A concept or object that appears within Unity to be the center or subject of its own world. The perception of being separate is a misidentification with a conceptual or 'made-up' subject. The separate individual is helplessly blind because it can only perceive from this self-absorbed center.

Cosmic Oomph:
This is the energy of spontaneous aliveness that can push us into Unity. It is an indescribable excitement or bliss-like energy, like Bliss Balls. It is a rapid bounce or drive, a snap of dynamic energy, a whip of spirit, a burst of gas, a sha-pow, ka-bam or zippiness.

Visit Paramananda at:

www.paramanandaishaya.com

To learn more about the practice of the Bright Path visit:

www.thebrightpath.com

MANTRA
BOOKS

We publish books on Eastern religions and philosophies.
Books that aim to inform and explore the various
traditions, that began rooted in East and
have migrated West.